To Love and to Cherish

(*For Engaged Couples*)

The Marriage Manual
of
The United Methodist Church

The Methodist Publishing House, Nashville, Tennessee

TO LOVE AND TO CHERISH

MANUFACTURED BY THE PARTHENON PRESS AT
NASHVILLE, TENNESSEE, UNITED STATES OF AMERICA

Foreword

To Couples Planning to Be Married

This is the official marriage manual of The United Methodist Church, prepared by the General Board of Education under direction of the Program-Curriculum Committee. Some of the best qualified pastors and counselors in the church have been asked to serve as consultants in the preparation of this manual.

This is your book. We hope you will find it useful.

On pages 129-42 at the back of this book you will find some information blanks. One of these is "Wedding Information," and is to be filled out in consultation with your minister. There are two "Premarital Questionnaires" —one for each of you. Your minister may request that you tear these out, complete, and return them to him as soon as possible. (If he does not, you will find it helpful if each of you fills out the one for you alone; then compare your answers and discuss them with each other.) This will enable him to counsel with you more helpfully. He will be happy to confer with you, both before your wedding and afterward.

Even though you may be well informed on much that is discussed in this book, you will find it rewarding if both of you read each page—preferably together. List areas in which you have disagreement and write down any questions that you would like to discuss with your minister. He will help you find answers to your questions, or if he does not feel he can help you, he will refer you to a qualified advisor.

It is our hope that through the use of this book you will come to a better understanding of each other and of the wonderful and sacred relationship into which you are now entering.

Henry M. Bullock
General Secretary
Division of Curriculum Resources
General Board of Education

Acknowledgments

Appreciation is expressed to the following consultants who have reviewed manuscripts and given invaluable assistance at each stage in the preparation of this manual.

DONALD B. APP
Program Director, Rocky Mountain Conference
Denver, Colorado

MILO F. BENNINGFIELD
Pastor-Counselor, Family Guidance Center
Dallas, Texas

E. CRAIG BRANDENBURG
Associate Secretary, Division of Higher Education
General Board of Education
The United Methodist Church
Nashville, Tennessee

DAVID B. CHAMBERLAIN
Psychologist
La Jolla, California

CURTIS A. CHAMBERS
Editorial Director, General Church Periodicals
Park Ridge, Illinois

HOWARD J. CLINEBELL, JR.
Professor of Pastoral Counseling
School of Theology at Claremont
Claremont, California

5

HELEN F. COUCH
Formerly Editor, *The Christian Home*
Nashville, Tennessee

EUGENE M. FRANK
Bishop, Missouri Area
St. Louis, Missouri

FLORIDE MOORE GARDNER
Professor of Education
Woman's College of Georgia
Milledgeville, Georgia

WILLIAM H. GENNÉ
Coordinator, Marriage and Family Ministries
National Council of the Churches of Christ
New York, New York

C. STEDMAN GLISSON, JR.
Physician,
Atlanta, Georgia

IVERSON GRAHAM, JR.
Director, Pastoral Care and Counseling

South Carolina Conference
Florence, South Carolina

BERKLEY C. HATHORNE
Coordinator, Education and Training
Division of Special Mental Health Programs
National Institute of Mental Health
Rockville, Maryland

GERALD K. HILL
Associate Minister, First United Methodist Church
Counselor, Mental Health and Retardation Clinic
Fargo, North Dakota

HARVEY C. HOLLAND
Chaplain, United States Air Force
Korea

EDWARD B. HOLLENBECK
Pastor, First United Methodist Church
Benton, Arkansas

FRANCIS E. KEARNS
    Bishop, Ohio East Area
    Canton, Ohio

T. CECIL MYERS
    Pastor, First United
    Methodist Church
    Athens, Georgia

EVERETT W. PALMER
    Bishop, Portland Area
    Deceased

THOMAS J. PUGH,
    Professor of Pastoral
    Counseling
    Gammon Theological
    Seminary
    Atlanta, Georgia

PAUL G. SCHURMAN
    Director, Program in
    Pastoral Care and Coun-
    seling
    East Area of The Ohio
    East Area of The United
    Methodist Church
    Canton, Ohio

LEON SMITH
    Director of Ministries in

Marriage
General Board of Educa-
tion
The United Methodist
Church
Nashville, Tennessee

EDWARD D. STAPLES
    Formerly Director of
    Ministries to Parents
    General Board of Educa-
    tion
    The United Methodist
    Church
    Nashville, Tennessee

CHARLES W. STEWART
    Professor of Pastoral The-
    ology and Supervised
    Ministries
    Wesley Theological Sem-
    inary
    Washington, D.C.

TROY M. STRONG
    Pastor, Mason United
    Methodist Church
    Tacoma, Washington

7

JAMES S. THOMAS
  Bishop, Iowa Area
  Des Moines, Iowa

JOHN M. VAYHINGER
  Professor of Psychology
  and Pastoral Counseling
  The School of Theology
  Anderson College
  Anderson, Indiana

W. RALPH WARD
  Bishop, Syracuse Area
  Syracuse, New York

DE FORREST WIKSTEN
  Director, Methodist
  Counseling Ministry
  Dallas–Fort Worth
  Area
  Dallas, Texas

FOSTER J. WILLIAMS
  Area Counselor
  Indiana Area of The
  United Methodist
  Church
  Indianapolis, Indiana

BERNICE M. WRIGHT
  Dean, College of Home
  Economics
  Syracuse University
  Syracuse, New York

DONALD R. YOUNG
  Director of Marriage and
  Family Study and Coun-
  seling Center, Institute of
  Religion and Human
  Development
  Texas Medical Center
  Houston, Texas

Appreciation is also expressed to the many pastors in local churches who have tested this manual in manuscript form.

Contents

9

CHAPTER I

You Have Come to the Church

You have requested that your marriage be solemnized by a Christian minister. This, in itself, is a significant decision. You might have gone to a civil officer. Your decision to be married by a Christian minister means that you join a vast company of Christians of other generations.

Thousands of couples have stood before the altar of the church and in the same or similar words that you will use have sought the blessing of God upon their union. Being a part of this great company of believers should add to the excitement of the occasion and deepen the meaning of your marriage vows.

Your minister is concerned about you and the quality of your marriage. Because he is interested in you individually and as a couple, he would like to talk with you about the meaning of marriage and about your future. If you have not already done so, you will want to arrange for one or more appointments with him as soon as possible to discuss the meaning of Christian marriage, plans for your wedding, and your life together. The church recommends one or more conferences before marriage.

After the wedding your minister's interest in your marriage will continue. If difficulties arise, you should feel free to go to him immediately for help. Some ministers have more skill in marriage counseling than others, and if your minister feels that his training and experience have not equipped him to help you with your particular problem, he will recommend a marriage counselor or other competent professional. Should you move to another community, do not hesitate to find a new church and establish a good relationship with your new minister there.

Love in Christian Marriage

Do you want to face life together because you love each other very much? It is part of God's plan that men and women should come together in love. In the very first chapters of the Bible we read: "So God created man in his own image, in the image of God he created him; male and female he created them. And God blessed them" (Genesis 1:27-28). And: "Therefore a man leaves his father and mother and cleaves to his wife, and they become one flesh" (Genesis 2:24).

Marriage is a human institution in which men and women of all cultures participate in various ways. But marriage is more than a human institution. It is also a divine institution—a gift from God, a part of his divine plan. In Christian marriage you accept God's will for your lives and agree to live together as his children, doing his work in the world.

Traditionally Christians have believed in the marriage

12

of one man and one woman. They enter marriage with the expectation that it will last "so long as ye both shall live." While the church has made provision for dissolving a marriage in exceptional cases, Christians should enter marriage with the expectation that this is a permanent relationship.

Christian marriage is a democracy in which each person has a right to express his own views. Ideally there will be complementary qualities and mutuality. Each will protect the rights and privacy of the other. This does not mean, however, that there are not happy marriages in which one person takes stronger leadership in making decisions than the other. Many persons need to depend on another. Sometimes it is the husband and sometimes it is the wife who makes the major choices. Even in a democracy some persons are more assertive than others.

In Paul's famous thirteenth chapter of I Corinthians, he places love as the greatest of the three Christian virtues—faith, hope, and love. But love is more than obedience to the command, "Love one another." Love is a free choice, an opportunity, and love must be cultivated if it is to grow.

Today a computer can choose a mate for you by sorting out like characteristics and common interests, but this is no special guarantee of a happy marriage. You, however, have made a thoughtful and deliberate choice. You may have prayed about this choice and feel that it is God's will that you marry. You feel that you care so much for each other that you want to belong to each other (not possessed but freely given) for the rest of your lives.

More Than a Legal Contract

Your marriage will be not just a legal contract, then. It will be a Christian commitment to each other and to God. If you feel that you are marrying in accordance with God's will, this does not mean that you will be spared conflicts and problems, but that, together, you can face these conflicts and problems in the confidence that God will help you find adequate solutions.

Marriage is more than a physical or social union. It is the union of two persons, two children of God. Through mutual trust and faith you can achieve a sense of oneness that will affect every relationship of your lives together. It is natural that you desire to possess each other, but if one is truly in love, he does not wish to dominate or exploit the other.

It is hoped that your marriage will be a partnership in which each person respects the rights and privileges, the wishes and desires of the other in all relationships. For in marriage there must be trust and confidence. Skill in living together in harmony must be cultivated, and oneness in marriage will come only through practice—love can grow or it can die.

Since there are no perfect marriages, forgiveness is an important element of the marriage relationship. When one person makes decisions that hurt the other, discussion, penitence, and forgiveness are called for. Just as God forgives his children when they make mistakes, so men and women in marriage must learn to forgive each other and try again.

Unity is another essential element in the marriage

relationship. Here is the possibility for developing a higher degree of intimacy than in any other adult human relationship. Physically and spiritually you can give yourselves to each other until "the two shall become one." This does not mean that you give up your own personality, but that two personalities are blended in such a manner as to achieve a sense of unity. Unity comes as each supplies what the other has not. This requires courage and trust as well as the ability to give and to take in love.

In a Christian marriage God enters into the union in a very real way. You are conscious of his presence. All of marriage becomes sacred. It has been suggested by some that there is really no such thing as Christian marriage, but rather Christians in marriage. We use the term *Christian marriage* here to mean a marriage in which husband and wife try to live in the spirit of Jesus Christ.

Christians believe "God is love" as revealed through Jesus Christ. We acknowledge God to be the creator and ruler of our lives, and in the wedding service we come to bow before him in reverence and humility, seeking his blessing upon our marriage. The service of holy matrimony is a religious service in which all who are present participate.

The Wedding

As we think about the meaning of Christian marriage, let us turn to the ritual that will be followed for your wedding. This ritual was approved by the General Con-

15

ference of The United Methodist Church and is essentially the ritual used by many other denominations. It has had only minor changes through the years.

You will want to study the ritual carefully. Some may want to memorize it so that they will be free to participate more fully in the ceremony, rather than concentrate on answering the questions.

You will be standing before God and a congregation of Christian witnesses to express your intentions regarding marriage. You and your friends will be celebrating your marriage in this service of worship.

In the opening paragraph of the service the minister will remind you that marriage is an "honorable estate, instituted of God," and therefore is not to be entered into hurriedly or without thought, "but reverently, discreetly, and in the fear of God."

Dearly beloved, we are gathered together here in the sight of God, and in the presence of these witnesses, to join together *this man and this woman* in holy matrimony; which is an honorable estate, instituted of God, and signifying unto us the mystical union which exists between Christ and his Church; which holy estate Christ adorned and beautified with his presence in Cana of Galilee. It is therefore not to be entered into unadvisedly, but reverently, discreetly, and in the fear of God. Into this holy estate these two persons come now to be joined. If any man can show just cause why they may not lawfully be joined together, let him now speak, or else hereafter forever hold his peace.

The minister will then read the charge to you to "now declare . . . your pledge of faith, each to the other,"

16

reminding you that if you keep the vows of matrimony and, together, endeavor to do God's will, "God will bless your marriage, will grant you fulfillment in it, and will establish your home in peace." Christian marriage is founded on love and on the expectancy of keeping promises.

I require and charge you both, as you stand in the presence of God, before whom the secrets of all hearts are disclosed, that, having duly considered the holy covenant you are about to make, you do now declare before this company your pledge of faith, each to the other. Be well assured that if these solemn vows are kept inviolate, as God's Word demands, and if steadfastly you endeavor to do the will of your heavenly Father, God will bless your marriage, will grant you fulfillment in it, and will establish your home in peace.

Next, the minister will call each of you by name and ask you individually to express your intentions in marriage as follows:

————, wilt thou have this woman (man) to be thy wedded wife (husband), to live together in the holy estate of matrimony? Wilt thou love her (him), comfort her (him), honor and keep her (him), in sickness and in health; and forsaking all other keep thee only unto her (him) so long as ye both shall live?

The response to the minister's questions is, "I will," expressing a commitment—an act of the will. In the marriage service each of you pledges to the other before

17

God to love, honor, and take care of the other and to remain true to each other. This vow is much stronger than a contract, which might easily be broken. This is your statement of belief in a one-man-one-woman relationship in which you agree to be true to each other "as long as ye both shall live."

There can be no doubt that the New Testament and the Christian faith regard marriage as a lifelong commitment on the part of husband and wife. The vows taken during the wedding service are clear. You expect that death alone will break the vow and covenant which you make in this service. As a Christian, you enter marriage expecting it to be a lasting experience.

When the minister asks the question, "Who giveth this woman to be married to this man?" it is usually the father of the bride who answers, "I do." A brother or other male relative may substitute for the father if this is necessary. In many weddings nowadays, however, the father will reply, "Her mother and I do."

Following the father's answer, the bride and groom join right hands and the groom repeats the following after the minister:

I, _____, take thee, _____, to be my wedded wife, to have and to hold, from this day forward, for better, for worse, for richer, for poorer, in sickness and in health, to love and to cherish, till death us do part, according to God's holy ordinance; and thereto I pledge thee my faith.

The bride then makes the same vow to the groom. Note the democratic nature of these vows.

Have you thought what it means to accept a person "for better, for worse, for richer, for poorer, in sickness and in health"? This means you accept each other as you are. You know that each of you has some faults, and you may think these will be outgrown or that you can change them after you are married, but do not count on it. Be prepared, instead, to love and accept each other just as you are.

Certainly there will be times when you are short of money. One or both of you may be out of a job. One or the other of you may have a long period of illness, or other difficulties may arise. Can you still love each other in such crises and face your problems together?

The minister now takes the ring from the best man and says:

The wedding ring is the outward and visible sign of an inward and spiritual grace, signifying to all the uniting of this man and this woman in holy matrimony, through the Church of Jesus Christ our Lord.

Then the minister may say:

Let us pray.
Bless, O Lord, the giving of these rings, that they who wear them may abide in thy peace and continue in thy favor; through Jesus Christ our Lord. Amen.

Or, if there is only one ring, the minister says:

Bless, O Lord, the giving of this ring, that he who gives it and she who wears it may abide forever in thy peace, and continue in thy favor; through Jesus Christ our Lord. Amen.

The minister then gives the ring to the man to put upon the third finger of the woman's left hand. The man, holding the ring there, says after the minister:

In token and pledge of our constant faith and abiding love, with this ring I thee wed, in the name of the Father, and of the Son, and of the Holy Spirit. Amen.

If there is a second ring, the minister gives it to the woman to put upon the third finger of the man's left hand, and holding the ring there, she says after the minister:

In token and pledge of our constant faith and abiding love, with this ring I thee wed, in the name of the Father, and of the Son, and of the Holy Spirit. Amen.

A ring, being a complete unbroken circle, is a symbol of the unity of marriage. It represents the full, beautiful, and endless love of a happy marriage. On the finger it is a constant reminder of the vows taken in the presence of God. By this act of giving and receiving the ring, you make your statement of marriage before the congregation. The minister, who will now pronounce you husband and wife, is both the representative of the state and a priest of God. He will say:

Forasmuch as _____ and _____ have consented together in holy wedlock, and have witnessed the same before God and this company, and thereto have pledged their faith each to the other, and have declared the same by joining hands and by giving and receiving *rings*; I pronounce that they are husband and wife together, in the name of the Father, and of the Son, and of the Holy Spirit. Those whom God hath joined together, let not man put asunder. Amen.

Then the minister asks the husband and wife to kneel and he prays:

O eternal God, creator and preserver of all mankind, giver of all spiritual grace, the author of everlasting life: Send thy blessing upon this man and this woman, whom we bless in thy name; that they may surely perform and keep the vow and covenant between them made, and may ever remain in perfect love and peace together, and live according to thy laws.

Look graciously upon them, that they may love, honor, and cherish each other, and so live together in faithfulness and patience, in wisdom and true godliness, that their home may be a haven of blessing and a place of peace; through Jesus Christ our Lord. Amen.

Still kneeling, the couple now joins with the minister and congregation in the Lord's Prayer. Since this is their first act of worship together as husband and wife, many feel it is more appropriate for them to pray the prayer with the congregation than have it sung as a solo.

Our Father, who art in heaven, hallowed be thy name. Thy kingdom come, thy will be done on earth as it is in heaven. Give us this day our daily bread. And forgive us our trespasses, as we forgive those who trespass against us. And lead us not into temptation, but deliver us from evil. For thine is the kingdom, and the power, and the glory, forever. Amen.

The minister now pronounces the benediction, a traditional form of blessing:

God the Father, the Son, and the Holy Spirit bless, preserve, and keep you; the Lord graciously with his favor look upon you, and so fill you with all spiritual benediction and love that you may so live together in this life that in the world to come you may have life everlasting. Amen.

Following the benediction, the bride and groom may kiss each other before they turn and leave the altar. It is appropriate that this symbol of affection be given for the first time in marriage before the altar and in the presence of the congregation.

A New Life Together

Christian marriage is a joy and a privilege, but it is also a distinct responsibility. The vows which you take include a commitment to love, honor, and comfort each other. Like a delicate plant, your love must be nourished and tended or it will die. Through tender, loving thoughtfulness of each other and a continuing effort toward good communication, you can keep your love growing and it will become more beautiful than you ever dreamed it could be. Here is your opportunity for a new life together. May the blessing of God be with you.

CHAPTER II

Are You Ready for Marriage?

You are now planning to launch out on the greatest pilgrimage of your life. We have already given some consideration to the meaning of Christian marriage and examined the vows that you will be asked to take. It is suggested that you further analyze your love, your motives for marriage, the gifts you bring to marriage, and your religious background. It is also suggested that you look at some of the problems you may have to confront. The questions that follow are intended to help you discuss these areas of concern with each other and with your minister.

What do you really know about marriage?
What responsibilities are you assuming?
Are you mature enough for marriage? What is maturity?
Do you understand the emotional forces that have caused you to be attracted to each other?
Do you have common interests?
Are your home backgrounds similar?
How have your home experiences influenced what you expect in marriage?
What do you believe really counts in life?

Can you afford to get married?

Are sexual interests and compulsion your primary reasons for getting married?

Do you have a common interest in religion?

Can you be tactfully and lovingly honest with each other?

Questions of this kind may come up in the days before the wedding. You may find yourself wondering if you know each other well enough for the intimacies of marriage. Most of the time, however, you will be quite sure that you want to be married.

Probably your questions and doubts will disappear as you go forward with your wedding plans. If fears and doubts are strong, however, they should be discussed frankly and honestly with your minister. He may be able to help you think through your questioning and decide whether these are simply normal doubts or whether it would be better to wait a while before marriage.

These questions may help you in getting to the real reason for your doubts:

Are you marrying because everyone else is and you feel it is the thing to do?

Are you marrying to get away from home and parents and responsibility?

Are you seeking a parental figure, a kind father or a loving mother?

Is your marriage a rebound from a previous love affair?

Have you been in love before? What do you understand by "love"?

Are you considering only your own selfish interests or are you considering the interests of the other person?

Are you marrying out of pity for the other person or in an effort to solve his or her problems? Do you want to reform the person you are marrying?

Is marriage the best possible relationship for both of you?

Have you gone together long enough and taken sufficient time to carefully consider what is before you, or is this a hasty marriage?

Are you sure of each other's love?

Most persons come to marriage with questions. Those listed above may suggest some reasons for discord in your future life together. Although it is not necessary that everything be perfect before you marry, it is wise to recognize and discuss the possibility of problems in marriage so that when and if they do arise you will not be overcome by them. You will be able to say to each other, "We knew this might happen. Let's face it, accept it, and see what we can do about it."

Why Are You Getting Married?

Here, arranged as a questionnaire, are some reasons why people get married. You may find this device helpful in examining your motives.

Rank by number in the appropriate column the five reasons that you feel are most true for you. Then cover up your answers and ask your partner to check his or her answers. Place a 1 after your first reason, 2 after the second most important reason, and so forth. Compare your answers and see if you agree on most of them.

Be honest with each other. Do not write in what you think might be expected by the other person. If you do have differences, it is best to discover them now.

	(Man)	(Woman)
1. Because everyone else is	———	———
2. To get away from home and parents	———	———
3. To find companionship	———	———
4. To avoid responsibility	———	———
5. Because I have been jilted by another	———	———
6. Because it is expected	———	———
7. Because we are in love	———	———
8. To have children	———	———
9. To have a home of my own	———	———
10. To find love	———	———
11. Because I want security	———	———
12. Because I'm afraid of never marrying	———	———
13. Because of sexual attraction	———	———
14. Because I think we are well suited to each other	———	———
15. Because I'm tired of the competition of others	———	———
16. Because of guilt over sexual experiences or pregnancy	———	———
17. To have a "father" or "mother" to love and care for me	———	———
18. To improve my present situation	———	———

Are You in Love?

How do you know you are really in love? Today you may feel you are sure, but you have probably been in love before.

When you were in grade school you showed interest in the other sex by teasing, showing off, and perhaps walking home with someone special. At times you probably selected the one you liked best to go with to group parties, or basketball games, or the movies. You wanted someone to want you. Later you may have "gone steady" with a special person. In all these experiences there were probably times when you felt you were in love.

Early love may be primarily infatuation and glamour. If so, it usually wears off and a deeper relationship is developed later. Sincere love may result from early relationships, however.

When you were growing up, you loved your parents and responded to their love for you. You still love your parents, but now you are seeking something more. You want a different kind of love in marriage.

In English we have only one word for many kinds of love, but the Greeks had three. *Philia* is used in the New Testament to mean "to regard with warm affection." This is a high quality of love expressed in companionship and mutual sharing, giving as well as receiving. We experience this love in the joy of merely being together, talking together, doing things together. It is the love of friendship and of family.

Another Greek word for love is *eros*, a desire for someone or something. This word is not used in the New

Testament. It usually refers to the sexual aspect of love which includes more than the physical. One of the powerful forces that draw men and women together is *eros*, or sexual love, a very important, God-given desire. It is a part of God's plan for the continuing of life. As we understand the meaning of sex today, this kind of love can be a source of deep and strong fulfillment in marriage. It can be an expression of a very tender, devout love between husband and wife. If a couple can find satisfaction and fulfillment in their sexual life in the early years of marriage, *eros* can mean a lifelong, enduring romance.

For the highest kind of love, the Greeks used the word *agape*. This is the word used in the New Testament statement, "Greater love [*agape*] has no man than this, that a man lay down his life for his friends" (John 15:13). This is the love that results in outgoing service to others. In marriage *agape* is the deep love which manifests itself in concern for the other person. *Agape* is not self-centered, but self-giving. It enables marriage partners to endure the inevitable crises and heartbreaks of life with a sense of the divine.

All three kinds of love are found simultaneously in Christian marriage. All are kept in delicate balance by *agape*.

No doubt you feel that you could never be more in love than you are at this moment, but a year from now it will be quite different. Love is dynamic. It may grow, but it may also die.

After your first year of marriage you will have learned how to adjust to each other better and you will have discovered many little ways to make each other happy. You will know each other's strengths and weaknesses and how you can supplement these. You will also have learned more about the satisfaction of each other's needs, and you will have discovered more of what to expect from each other. You will no longer fear competition from others, and there should be less fear in your love than now. You should have a deeper and more secure sense of oneness. You may also have found out that some of your expectations of marriage have not been realized and that you are disappointed about some things.

Some persons are disappointed in marriage because they have entirely unrealistic expectations. They expect married life to be an exciting, day-after-day romance—a continuing love feast, an extension and intensification of the high moments of courtship. Their expectations are fantasies drawn from portrayals of love in romantic novels, television, and movies. Entering a marriage with such expectations is an almost certain route to failure for there is nothing of self-giving love here, no mutual desire for a true understanding between persons, and no commitment to common goals and purposes.

Engagement has been a time of exploration for you. You have found new depths in your relationships with each other. Probably you have found greater emotional security. You have discovered likes and dislikes and personal habits which you may not have noticed before. During your engagement you have had an opportunity to decide whether or not you want to live with each other for the rest of your life.

29

In marriage, love may dwindle or even die, depending not only on the realism of your expectations, but on how much you are willing to give to keep it alive and growing. Love must be cultivated and strengthened from day to day. It calls for continued attention to its growth. You will need to work at developing responsible initiative, sharing responsibility, dealing with hostilities which may arise, and at the same time, cultivating the courtesies and consideration that have been a part of your relationship before marriage.

Premarital Intercourse

Sociological studies reveal that sexual intercourse before marriage is not uncommon. This does not make it either right or desirable, however. Often it is not a deliberately planned experience, but feelings become stronger than a couple can control.

Sexual intercourse may have occurred as an act of love during engagement. This may or may not create a strong sense of guilt. If you are troubled by guilt feelings, you may feel better about it if you talk over the matter privately with your minister. Everyone makes mistakes of one kind or another, but each of us can find forgiveness and a new life for ourselves. There is no need to keep on punishing yourself by dwelling upon past mistakes. We must learn to accept the consequences of our action, forgive each other, and accept God's love and forgiveness. Look to the future and try to make your marriage a successful one. (See also Chapter IV.)

What Do You Know About Each Other?

Relatively similar interests are far more important to a strong marriage than most people realize. The marriage of the princess and the pauper may be very romantic, but such a union can mean many difficult problems. If only one person is accustomed to luxury, what about standards of living after marriage? What will a higher standard of living mean to the person who has little or nothing—a turn to extravagant spending or pinch-penny saving, either of which could cause great unhappiness? Different economic backgrounds may be the cause of tensions for a married couple, but if differences are approached reasonably these can be resolved.

Important, too, are family backgrounds. Do you like your future in-laws? How do they feel about your marriage? Do you think they like you? It may be that you are not going to live near either family, but relatives do visit occasionally. Are you embarrassed while in their presence? In case of an emergency, could you welcome them into your home to live with you for a while? Actually, you marry each other's families much more than you realize.

We tend to pick up the attitudes and customs of those in our parental homes. A girl will very often cook and keep house as her mother does. She may have a similar temperament and will probably treat her husband much as her mother treated her father. A boy may be like his father in his attitudes toward his wife—domineering, attached to her as though she were his mother, or accept-

31

ing her lovingly as a full and equal partner in the marriage.

The father in the home also influences a daughter. It may be that a girl will expect her husband to be very much like her father and will be disappointed if he is not. Family characteristics and your feelings about each other's family should be talked over frankly before you are married.

It will help you understand each other if you know about each other's family background. Too often marriage counselors run into situations where friction has developed because one person has said nasty things about the other's relatives. You may not like each other's relatives, but you ought to try to understand them and be able to see if your spouse has some of his relatives' characteristics that are objectionable to you. Then try to remember he is also a person in his own right.

The home backgrounds from which you come need not be exactly alike, but it is important that you have some common interests growing out of these backgrounds. For example, if one of you likes music and the other does not, this may not be disturbing. But if one likes jazz and the other prefers symphonies, or if one has a great many cultural interests and the other does not, this may cause difficulty.

Do you like similar TV programs? books? recordings? magazines? hobbies? When you go out together, can you agree on the kind of entertainment you enjoy, or does one prefer to stay home and read while the other goes to sports events? You may or may not have much money to spend on recreation, but you are going to have to make decisions regarding the kind of recreation you will both enjoy. If you have enough other common interests, each of you may be able to participate in a different kind of recreation and simply admit that you like it this way.

Friends are important, too. Do you like your future wife's friends? Do they know you? She may want to have some of them visit in your home. It is hardly fair to ask her to give up her friends because she is marrying you, although she should not depend on them in the same way as before marriage. Will you like your husband's friends? Will he want to bring them home to meet you?

Do you argue about friendships before marriage? If so, what is the basis of your argument? Not having friends may mean that you are new to a community. Or it may mean that you are so shy or self-centered that you cannot get along with people. If this is the case with either of you, be sure that you understand the other's shyness or boldness.

Educational background may influence your choice of friends. Does your partner's incorrect use of English or lack of interest in education annoy you? Too much difference may give one person a feeling of inferiority and the other a feeling of superiority. By reading and studying, some of the differences in education may be overcome, but it will require continuing effort to overcome the incorrect use of the English language.

What About Values?

Differences in ideals and purposes are often a basic cause of friction and tension for couples. Do you agree as to the things that are important in life? Are you basically honest with each other? If one of you feels that the other is not, you will want to examine this aspect of your relationship carefully.

Being truthful does not mean that you have to tell all your inmost thoughts or confess every mistake you have ever made. And you must determine how much you can tell each other about former love affairs or sexual contacts. There is certainly no value for either of you in boasting about every date you had before marriage. You can be perfectly honest and still not bring up past experiences that may endanger the marriage.

If you have guilt feelings about things you have done in the past and you feel the need for confession, go to your minister or to a marriage counselor and get it out in the open. Confession to God may also be helpful.

Do both of you have the same basic concerns about persons? Are you interested in the same causes? If one is not sympathetic toward the other's church or community work, this could become a continuing source of friction.

Interfaith Marriages

Interfaith marriage is marriage between two persons of diverse religious background such as Catholic-Protestant, Catholic-Jewish, Protestant-Jewish. Sometimes, too, persons hold radically different theological points of view, such as modernist-fundamentalist, liberal-conservative, and sometimes a person of strong religious faith marries a person of no religious faith. If you belong to two different Protestant churches, your traditions may be a cause of conflict, but ordinarily there are no major differences in belief. Differences are primarily in regard to organization and ritual.

There are those who feel that real enrichment can come from an interfaith or intercultural marriage because each person has something unique to contribute to the marriage. This is possible if you have sufficient wisdom to emphasize the positive contributions which each can make rather than differences and will be easier if you live in an area where such marriages are accepted.

Normally it is better if you can agree on one faith or the other, holding some basic beliefs in common, so that you can attend church together and bring up your children in the same faith. It is important that you make a decision on the matter of religious observance before marriage rather than adding this as a stumbling block in the adjustments that come later.

Some ultra-conservative or ultra-liberal partners will not compromise, however. They will maintain that theirs is the only religion and, therefore, will continue in their beliefs after marriage. If the other partner has no definite convictions, he may be able to accept such an uncompromising position. If both feel strongly about the form of their religious faith, however, there is certain to be friction.

It has been estimated that there are about 100,000 Catholic-Protestant marriages in the nation every year and that such marriages are increasing rapidly. Both Catholics and Protestants have questions about these interfaith marriages. If at all possible, they want to avoid the danger of unhappiness and possible breakdown. *The Book of Resolutions of The United Methodist Church, 1968* says of mixed marriages, "Marriage, ideally, is a matter of responsible decision between two human beings who decide to share their lives, found a family, and probably enter into parenthood. The church, recognizing the value of each individual as a child of God, supports and blesses any marriage entered into with thoughtful consideration of the vows of marriage and the commitment which these vows entail. Moreover the church commits itself to fulfillment of its role as a supportive community that encompasses all families in its love and concern.

"Marriage inevitably reflects differences in backgrounds of the partners. But in our present-day pluralistic and ecumenical world, marriage is entered into increasingly by persons with different religious, racial, and ethnic backgrounds. Such differences may enrich family life, or they may lead to conflict, indifference, or even failure.

"It is important that those contemplating a mixed marriage explore both the cohesive and the divisive potentialities of their differences, examine their motivations, and realistically assess the durability of the marriage and the probable effect of social pressures on them and their children. Special consideration should be given to the traditions in which their children are to be reared. Pastors and other trusted persons can assist them in exploring the many facets of their lives that will be affected by a mixed marriage" (p. 92).

One reason Catholics, Protestants, and Jews are all concerned about mixed marriages is that many persons in such situations lose their interest in the church. Rather than argue about religious differences, they simply ignore them and try to avoid conflict through nonattendance.

Several reliable studies have indicated that there is greater possibility of divorce or separation in a mixed religious marriage than in a marriage in which both husband and wife have the same religious faith.

One of the greatest difficulties in an interfaith marriage may come in adjusting to the families involved. Some families care so much about their particular beliefs that they find it difficult to accept in-laws of a different faith. A few families feel so deeply about their religious beliefs that they consider one who marries outside their faith as no longer a part of the family.

"But I am not marrying his family," a bride protests during counseling. In a real sense, however, one does marry the whole family. A bride wants to be accepted and admired by her husband's family and is disappointed if she is not. A husband wants to be proud of the bride he brings home. He wants to know that she will be accepted and that there will be little friction in his home.

The chief problems that arise in an interfaith marriage are these:

1. *Religious pressure of parents and in-laws.* (See paragraphs above.)

2. *Family planning.* At the present time the use of any mechanical form of conception control is regarded as seriously sinful by the Roman Catholic Church. Some thoughtful Catholics are protesting, and this position is

37

under study. Many hope it may be changed. In the meantime, statistics indicate that Catholics do not have many more children than Protestants. However, if birth control methods other than the rhythm method approved by the Catholic Church are used, serious feelings of guilt may result. (See page 81 for a discussion of various methods of conception control.)

3. *Selecting a doctor.* Devout Roman Catholic physicians, when a crisis demands that a doctor decide whether to save the life of a mother or the child, believe that it is more desirable to save the life of the child than the life of the mother. Protestants cannot always subscribe to this point of view. Many Roman Catholic physicians will not prescribe contraceptive measures other than the rhythm method.

4. *Children's religious training.* Some studies indicate that children generally go to the church of the mother in spite of the fact that a couple married by a priest may have promised to bring up their children as Catholics. A couple is no longer always required to sign a statement agreeing to bring up their children in the Catholic Church as was formerly the case. An oral agreement is all that is now required in some parishes. Nevertheless, the Catholic is still expected to promise to bring up the children in the Roman Catholic Church if the couple is married by a priest.

It is now possible for a Protestant minister to participate in a Catholic wedding by giving his blessing after the couple has been pronounced man and wife by the priest. A Catholic priest must have special permission to assist in a Protestant marriage service. While the growing spirit of ecumenicity has brought many changes, it has not solved all the problems of interfaith marriage.

5. *Culture.* There are still many differences between Catholics and Protestants related to cultural background, and these may cause difficulties. For example, some Protestants make sacrifices during Lent while others do not; a devout Catholic is conscientious in his observance of Lent. Protestants may serve baked ham for supper on Friday night, but Orthodox Jews may not partake and some Roman Catholics would feel that it was wrong. The Roman Catholic Church places strong emphasis upon obedience to the authority of the Church.

If you are considering an interfaith marriage, it is important that you become aware of the many ways in which your differing backgrounds will affect your marriage. You may feel that you can adjust, that your love is strong enough to withstand the pressures. And it may be. But your differences will be less disturbing if both partners are prepared to examine them with sincere respect for each other's point of view.

Basically you need to decide whether you and the members of both families have (1) almost no interest in religion, (2) some interest, or (3) a great deal of interest. Visit each other's churches, talk with both sets of parents, and ask for a series of counseling interviews with the priest, rabbi, or minister. Think through your religious differences and try to see what effect these differences have on your marriage.

If agreement about religion cannot be reached before marriage, there is little hope for agreement afterward. It is easy to say, "We will worry about our children's religion when the time comes." The time has come long before your children are born. It is far better to settle your differences before marriage.

If you are considering an interfaith marriage, here are some suggestions:

1. Talk it over with your parents. Will all of them give their blessing? If not, are you prepared to go ahead, knowing your marriage will make them unhappy or antagonistic?

2. Do not try to cover up your differences. Discuss them frankly. List both points of agreement and disagreement. Can any of these be compromised? If you feel it would be helpful, invite your minister or other trusted person to talk with you.

3. Consider the advisability of joining a third church together if it is impossible for you to agree on one church or the other.

4. Agree never to criticize the religion of your partner or to argue about religion before your children.

5. Decide not to boast about the superiority of your particular brand of religion. Do your best to live as you feel a Christian should.

How About Money?

The amount of money you have will not determine your happiness, but financial responsibility is important to a marriage. When couples manage their monetary affairs responsibly, they are surprised at how much they can achieve with limited resources. On the other hand, when money is mismanaged, tension is inevitable, regardless of the size of your income.

Like sex and religion, money may not be the real difficulty in an adjustment to marriage, but disagreements over money may become a concealment for deeper conflict. It takes money to live, but the amount of cash on hand is not nearly so important as the values, goals, and methods of decision-making that determine the way it is used.

A man who has a steady job and adequate training knows that he will probably be able to support his wife and future family. A couple may not have much money now, but if they can use good judgment in spending what they have, they will be able to handle a larger income later in life.

Will the Wife Be Employed?

Many young couples begin life today with the conveniences their parents acquired only after years of marriage. They feel that it is necessary to have a nice apartment, an automobile, a television set, money for vacations, and so forth. To make all this possible, two incomes are needed, so many wives plan to work outside the home at least until the children come.

The typical couple starts out in a small apartment with a good deal of comfort and with two incomes. Having prepared for a career, many women will want to follow their career for a few years before having children. Some will wish to pick it up again after the children are old enough to be left at home or at school.

41

In a large percentage of marriages, however, children come within the first year. This throws the budget, based on two incomes, out of balance. At first glance, it seems that nine months will be time enough to save for a baby, but the months pass quickly, and with costs constantly going up many couples are not ready. Even though they agree that it is sensible to plan well in advance for the coming of children and to be financially ready for their arrival, many couples never actually work out an adequate plan.

In one recent study about two thirds of the couples interviewed indicated that they had experienced financial stress in marriage. If wives are constantly nagging their husbands for more money or if husbands are spending money as though they had only one person to support, tensions are certain to arise.

Sometimes conflict arises, too, because a wife earns more money than her husband. This means that if she has to take time off for pregnancy, there is a considerable loss of income. Also, there is the question of whether or not she will go back to work after a child is born. Some people feel very strongly about this. Many men feel that "a woman's place is in the home" and she ought to stay at home at least until the children are old enough to enter school.

Numerous studies have been made of the family life of working mothers. These studies indicate that it is possible to have a healthy family life and to raise children who are not delinquents even though both father and mother are working. Success in marriage and parenthood is not assured just because a mother stays at home. Personal characteristics of the mother and the father, the amount and the quality of time spent together in the family, and the kind of supervision and guidance which parents provide for their children seem to be the important factors whether both parents work or not. It is the quality of family living rather than the amount of time a family spends together that is important, both in the relationships between husbands and wives and between parents and children.

Working out a spending plan together before marriage will help you discover whether you see eye to eye regarding priorities in handling money. Try keeping an account of what you spend day by day. At the end of the month total up what each of you has spent and go over your accounts together. Now estimate the additional expenses you will have when married and write these into a tentative budget. Begin with such fixed items as rent, food, insurance, giving, and regular payments. Make allowance for possible emergencies. List your long-range goals for saving and spending.

"Two can live as cheaply as one" is merely an expression of wishful thinking. If you have been paying for two apartments, eating most of your meals out, or spending a good deal on entertainment, you may be able to cut down considerably. But if either of you has been living at home and your parents have been paying the bills, you may not know exactly how much you do spend. It will strengthen your marriage if you agree now to work out major expenditures together.

Do you have school debts or other obligations that should be paid off before marriage? If you cannot pay them immediately, get them out in the open so that you can look at them together and know what obligations you may have for the future. Are either or both of you planning for further education? Consider this, too, in developing your spending plan.

How Much—For What?

Here are some suggested percentages for a budget:

Income Taxes 14%
Food and Meals Out 20%
Housing 17%
Household Operation 5%
Clothing, Cleaning, and Repairs 7%
Transportation and Car Expense 9%
Medical and Dental Care 4%
Insurance and Savings 5%
Personal, Barber and Beauty Shop, etc. 2%
Recreation, Vacations, Newspapers, Magazines,
    and Books 4%
Contributions to Church and Community Charities ...10%
Miscellaneous 3%
_____
100%

As your income increases you can afford a larger percentage for some of these items, but remember that you will also pay a larger percentage for income taxes. If you still have educational expenses or debts, these have a prior claim on your budget and you will have to adjust accordingly. The amount allowed for contributions to churches and charities is larger than average for United

States citizens, but may not be as much as you feel you ought to give. Include contributions in your budget so that you will not be guilty of giving only leftovers.

While you are working on a spending plan, why not work on a possible budget for a house of your own, if this is in your planning? You should review this at least every three to six months, making changes and adjustments.

Handling money is often a problem in marriage, but it need not be if each person trusts the other and if both know where the money goes. Each person needs some money for personal items, such as gifts and incidental spending, for which he does not need to account, but by sharing responsibility in the overall handling of finances it is possible to avoid the problem that arises when one partner feels the other spends more than his share.

More for Your Money

Some people seem to get a great deal more out of a small income than others. By taking advantage of weekend specials, comparing prices, waiting for seasonal sales, and by avoiding excessive interest rates for credit, they are able to get more value for their money.

Many heartaches in marriage come from unwise use of credit. It is normally better to buy small gifts for each other rather than spending money you do not have to purchase on an installment plan. It seems so easy to buy through installment financing, either with department store or bank credit cards, and many Americans always live ahead of their salaries.

45

Some large items, such as a house or a car or a refrigerator, you may have to purchase on credit. Credit rates vary. Where bank rates used to be pegged at 6 percent, now they vary from 6 to 10 percent and occasionally 12 percent. Credit unions generally charge 1 percent per month on the unpaid balance which averages out about 6 percent if paid within a year. Consumer finance companies and small loan laws can make a charge as high as 30 percent. In many states the maximum rate for installment buying is 1½ percent per month on the remaining balance. If you keep continuing your balance, this may be as much as 18 percent or more if the state law permits. Therefore if you save your money in advance and pay cash, you will have eighteen dollars more on every hundred to spend or to save.

Some stores will allow you to buy on a three-payment plan—thirty, sixty, or ninety days—without paying any additional finance charges. It pays to investigate the rate you are paying and then decide whether you want to pay the additional amount of interest. Or is it better to wait a few months and pay cash?

If you find yourself overly involved in installment buying, talk to a banker or other financial counselor and work out a plan for getting out from under your load of debt. As you begin your married life together, it is a good plan not to buy more than you can pay for in thirty or sixty days.

Several studies on family life have indicated that money is frequently ranked first by young couples as the cause of family friction. One study of 391 wives with high school education indicated that 26 percent of them had money difficulties. In a list of seven causes of friction a larger percentage checked money than any of the other items, which were ranked in the following order[1]:

1. Money
2. Children
3. Recreation
4. Personality

5. In-laws
6. Roles
7. Religion—politics—sex

College graduates had fewer problems with money but more problems with the care of their children.

In Conclusion

Some people feel that "like marries like"; others, that "opposites attract." After reading through this chapter you may feel that having many things in common makes for greater compatibility in marriage. This is true; but the fact that you are different—one a man and the other a woman—has brought you together and is the basis of your physical union. You have a lifetime ahead to find out about each other, to work together at reinforcing your likenesses and understanding your differences.

In this chapter we have tried to look at some of the problems of marriage and your readiness to meet these problems. It is not the purpose of this manual to scare you out of your intention to be married, but to help you recognize that there are potential areas of difficulty which, if recognized and discussed before your wedding, may save you many heartaches during your married life.

[1] From *Husbands and Wives*, by Robert O. Blood, Jr., and Donald M. Wolfe (The Free Press, 1960), p. 244.

Chapter III

A Growing Partnership

Marriage is a covenant relationship, not a contract. It is a covenant on the part of two people in the sight of God and the church to live together "for better, for worse, for richer, for poorer, in sickness and in health, to love, and to cherish, till death us do part."

This covenant applies to many different kinds of situations. For example, there will be times when you feel happy and quite content with your relationship to each other. At other times married life will not run smoothly, and you may even question whether you should have taken the step in the first place. This does not mean that you should give up your marriage and try again with someone else. It may mean merely that you need to give more attention to each other and to cultivating your relationship.

A wedding is the beginning of a marriage but not the guarantee of its success. However, if both of you have a strong desire to succeed, if you trust and depend on each other and work together, you can achieve a life of fulfillment for both of you.

What are your goals or expectations? As has already been said, if you are looking for perfect bliss in marriage, you will be disappointed. One of the advantages in the arranged marriages of some cultures is that couples are not so likely to look at marriage through rose-colored glasses. As they enter marriage they hope, plan, and work for love, and love often results. Parents, in arranging a marriage, have probably been concerned that the couple come from similar backgrounds and will work together well in partnership. In this kind of marriage, love grows and develops as the result of hope and work. The couple does not enter marriage with the expectation that love alone will solve all their problems.

Do not expect each other to be perfect. Neither of you is perfect before marriage, and you probably will not be afterward. If you expect to discover some faults in each other, you will be neither surprised nor disappointed. If you anticipate some difficulties, and recognize that these are normal, you have made a good beginning for solving any difficulties that may arise later.

Need to Understand Roles

There are important biological and psychological differences between men and women. They complement each other and are so glandularly constructed that they respond emotionally to each other. This is a part of the divine plan.

You bring to marriage not only these physical and psychological differences but also certain mental images of what a husband and a wife ought to be. Such images have been determined by community attitudes and customs as well as by what each of you has observed in your parental home.

49

If a husband and wife think pretty much alike about the place, or role, of men and women in marriage, they will have fewer problems of adjustment. Even so, in this day of changing values and customs, you will probably experience some confusion. If, however, backgrounds have been quite different and understanding of the role of men and women in marriage is not at all similar, each will have different expectations and both will probably experience a great deal of role confusion.

Changes taking place in our time and culture today are bringing us to a new view of roles in marriage. As people have moved from rural situations to an urban life, the place of men and women in the family has been altered.

In a rural or small town situation, wives and children had firsthand knowledge of what the father did to earn a living. His wife and children saw him daily at his work. They understood why he was tired at night. His role as a provider was clear to all.

A woman's work was also clearly delineated. Her job was to care for the children, prepare the meals, keep the house, and possibly to work in the garden. She was expected to fit into her husband's plans, have meals ready on time, keep his clothes mended and clean. There was time at mealtime and in the early evening for the family to relax and enjoy one another. On Sundays they went to church together. When each did what was expected, there was a minimum of difficulty.

The move to the cities and technological advances that have come so rapidly in our society have greatly changed the pace and style of family living. Many services once performed in the home are now no longer necessary

50

or are handled mechanically. The work week for men has been shortened. No longer is it necessary for women to spend all their time sewing, canning, cooking, washing, scrubbing, or supervising a small garden of foodstuffs for use in the home. Today a homemaker may work outside the home or have a wide variety of social or church and community activities, which makes quite a difference in what is expected of her by her husband and family.

A girl who has been brought up in a home where all the work was done by servants will have a concept of the wife's role that is quite different from that of a girl who has lived in a home where she has helped with all the housework.

If a man comes from a home where his mother worked all day outside the home and was considerably rushed to get meals at the close of the day, and if his father helped with the housework, this gives him one picture of family life. If, on the other hand, Father never did any work around the house and felt it was "woman's work" to dust and clean, prepare the meals and wash the dishes, his son has still another concept of family life. In marriage, this young man may frequently recall the good pies and cakes his mother used to bake or refer to her ability as a manager of the home. He will find it difficult to adjust his image of a homemaker to a working wife who comes home each night tired from work and maybe a little cross.

His wife may have received something of her ideal of a man's role from her father or from her brothers. This image of what a husband ought to be may not match with her partner's image of himself as a husband.

Traditional male and female roles are much confused today, and each couple must work through to solutions regarding what each person will do in the home. A woman is no less a woman because she likes to fish or cut the grass. Nor is a man less a man because he helps with the housework, diapers the baby, or cooks. Recognize that times change, that job opportunities change, and that the role of men and women is constantly changing. Work out together the role each of you will assume in your home. If you disagree, talk it out and try to reach a solution.

Need for Acceptance as a Person

Every individual needs to be recognized for what he is and to be respected as a person. A creative marriage does not stifle but enhances individuality. If individual personality differences were not recognized in the parental home, either partner may overcompensate by trying to become the dominant personality in the new family relationship. This can mean that this partner does not recognize the other person's rights and privileges as a person.

When she marries, a woman gives up her own and assumes her husband's surname. But she does not cease to be the person she was before marriage. Healthy self-regard is a must for her, as it is for everyone. As husband and wife recognize the importance of this need in each other, each must continually work at building up the other's self-esteem.

For example, remarks that belittle a person's importance are devastating, especially in the presence of others. On the other hand, when a husband boasts about his wife's cooking either in private or in public, it builds up her esteem. If she praises his ability to get along with people or to make a special contribution in his work, this gives him a sense of importance.

Look for and express appreciation for the good points in each other. And learn to understand and accept each other's weaknesses.

The Need to Be Loved and Wanted

Men and women turn to each other because of a basic need for intimacy and closeness. Each person has a need to love and to be loved, to feel that he is giving himself and at the same time is desired by someone else. We can find such intimacy in marriage.

Sex is an expression of love, but it is only a part of love. Important also may be the desire for companionship with someone who really cares, and for children to love and care for. One shares his interests, his desires, his hopes, his fears, and his love with another in the intimacy of marriage and the home.

If persons do not find this love at home, they often seek it outside through excessive involvement in clubs or groups of various kinds. An overinvolvement in one's work or in the activities of his church may represent an attempt to satisfy persistent needs for love, respect, and achievement of a sense of personal identity. Neither religious nor fraternal relationships or professional achievement, however, can fully compensate for the unsatisfied need to love and be loved within the family.

A person needs to be loved not only when he does well but also when he fails. If hopes for success and some of the economic blessings of life do not materialize, many men and women quite naturally experience a sense of failure. In marriage, however, a person hopes to be loved for what he is, not for his attainments or because he fits the ideal image of a marriage partner. In the close intimacy of marriage the individual's life can grow and develop, becoming stronger and finer than it was before. The knowledge that we are loved for what we are helps us to cope with whatever problems arise.

It is important to recognize, too, that there are some things about each of us that cannot be changed even though we may desire to do so. Accepting a husband for what he is, accepting a wife for what she is, means that neither tries to change the other.

The Need for Privacy

While everyone needs love and intimacy, everyone also needs privacy. This is sometimes hard to come by in the small rooms and apartments available to newly married couples today. If either husband or wife desires privacy, the other should respect that desire, accepting this characteristic as a part of the other's being a person. All barriers do not have to come down in order to have intimacy.

Respect the privacy of personal drawers or closets. If you do not want your wife going through your pockets or your husband going through your purse, frankly say so. Respect each other's right to receive personal mail, also. Read each other's letters only when invited to do so.

It is also wise to respect your partner's right to have some thoughts which are not shared. Do not coax for a sharing of those intimate thoughts which a person would rather keep to himself.

Some persons like privacy in the bathroom. If so, respect this preference. For instance, some find it annoying to find personal clothing draped around the bathroom, but others do not mind removing stockings and undergarments from the shower rod before taking a shower. Make sure you understand your partner's feelings about such matters and try to be accommodating.

Need for Friendships

Married couples will need friendships beyond the home. You undoubtedly have some friends in common with whom you get along famously, and you will want to maintain these friendships after marriage. But you will also need to develop friendships with other married couples.

A husband may have some friends whom his wife does not appreciate and vice versa. A man still needs some male companionship, and for a while may want to keep up some of the friendships with men he knew before marriage, but he will not need their company in the same way and perhaps not as often as formerly. A wife may need friendship with women she knew before marriage. Recognize, however, that these personal friends cannot always be shared.

55

Need for Communication

Simple as it sounds, it takes a great deal of effort and honest exploration if husbands and wives are to develop adequate communication. Before marriage they may have been able to talk to each other and appreciate each other. If there were things about each other which they did not completely understand, this mystery only added to the glamour of their relationship. But after marriage the need for real communication becomes more and more important.

"Ted just doesn't talk to me," said one bride of twelve months. "Before we were married we seemed to have a lot of things to talk about—school, friends, dates, parties —but now when he comes home at night, all he wants to talk about is his work. I've been home all day, cleaning house, washing dishes, taking care of the baby, and I'd like to get out and do something. But he says he's tired. We used to have good times together. Now when I suggest going out to dinner, all he says is, 'That costs money.' Will we ever have fun any more?"

What does Ted think when he comes home after a hard day's work?

"It certainly would be nice to stay home and read tonight, but Mary will probably want to go somewhere. We never seemed to have any trouble just talking, reading, and enjoying each other's company before we were married. Now all she talks about is the baby, the housecleaning, and the washing. The first few months things went pretty well. We both worked during the day, came home and got meals together, or went out for dinner occasionally. But since the baby came, Mary never seems to have any time for me. She wants to go bowling or over to Fred and Ethel's house. I never could stand Fred, but Mary seems to think he is pretty wonderful. We can't even seem to talk about it. I wonder what we'll argue about tonight."

Why are Mary and Ted having such a difficult time communicating with each other? Sometimes they blame it on the baby that came after they had been married less than a year. At first they thought it was wonderful to have their children early, and although the pregnancy was not planned, they accepted the idea of a baby and planned for it with a great deal of love and affection. When Mary could no longer work, however, their income was drastically reduced, and now they have some serious financial problems.

Each is trying to solve the difficulty of communication alone and does not seem to be able to understand the other's point of view. Sometimes they argue. At other times Ted tries the silent treatment. They seem to focus on the differences in their lives rather than trying to find points of agreement.

Both Ted and Mary really love their baby, and this might have been a basis upon which they could have strengthened their relationship. But sometimes Mary is sarcastic. This never seems to win an argument because Ted then comes back with a wisecrack about her family. They have never quite resorted to force, but their arguments are becoming more frequent. When really angry, Ted has a tendency to stamp his foot or throw down the book he is reading and go for a walk. He does not seem to realize that Mary needs a change from caring for the baby, that she needs love and sympathy just as he does. Nor is he sensitive to her need for rest and for companionship and love at the end of a busy day.

After arguments there is little sense of intimacy or desire for sexual love on Mary's part, although Ted seems to desire it even more, perhaps as a symbol of making up. There are times when they still seem to be in love, but during the day Mary wonders if Ted really does care about her any more. He no longer seems to give her as much time and attention as when they were first married.

Ted and Mary have not communicated their needs and feelings to each other. It would help if they could get their differences out in the open so they could begin to understand each other better. Or, if they could talk with their minister or a marriage counselor, he might help them find ways of resolving their difficulties.

Here are some of the barriers to valid communication in marriage. Which do you think were barriers for Ted and Mary?

False pride
Selfishness
Stubbornness
Role confusion
Inability to see the other's needs
Extreme aggressiveness
Misunderstanding of motives
Differences in background
Absorption in personal interests
Trivial differences of opinion

Lack of experience in communicating
Assumption that because one is happy, the other is also
Inability to accept each other's faults
Lack of awareness of one's own feelings and motivation
Hearing only words and overlooking feelings
Preoccupation with work or personal interests
Differences in values
Refusal to listen

Communication is the art of hearing and being heard. It may be both verbal and nonverbal. It has to do with both ideas and feelings. It involves openness, honesty, acceptance, and integrity. It requires talking things over. Husbands and wives need to develop the art of being good listeners. Dialogue is essential in a successful marriage. Here are some suggestions for better communication.

1. *Don't take each other for granted.* When you are happy, say so. Share your joy. Express appreciation for good cooking, little kindnesses, a good day's work well done, careful grooming, good times together. Strong, silent types do not contribute much to marriage.

2. *Try to understand the other's point of view.* Don't always take it for granted that you know what the other person is thinking. See that each of you has a chance to express your thinking, then try to understand the meaning of what is said. In the beginning each may blame the other for some misunderstanding, but as you talk it over, you may realize that both are involved and in some way responsible for the conflict.

3. *Think before you speak.* You know each other's strengths and weaknesses. It does not take long to learn

that there are some points at which your partner is very sensitive. Just because you are a little miffed about something, do not thrust in the knife and turn it at these tender spots. Once unkind words are spoken, they cannot be recalled and it is hard to patch up the damage done. Try to discover why you want to hurt each other, then make an honest effort to get rid of thinking and feelings that are causing the trouble.

4. *Look for points of agreement.* You may have much more in common than you think you have.

5. *Talk things over.* Life can become so involved and you may be so busy with petty things that you have no time for trying to understand each other. Plan for time to be alone. Wash dishes or do other tasks together. Take a walk. Money spent for a weekend away from home and the children is often well spent. Arrange some activities in which you can participate together so you will have something to talk about. You may want to plan deliberately to share particular experiences or some special reading material so that you will have some live topics of conversation.

6. *Don't use pressure to get your own way.* Shouting, physical force, sarcasm, silence, or using your age, education, or family background to pressure your partner into doing what you want can be disastrous. Such tactics may cause him to become defensive and shout back, or they may cause him to withdraw completely.

7. *Express your feelings.* If something is troubling you, do not keep it to yourself. But help your partner understand why you feel as you do. Try to sense his feelings about the situation.

8. *Ask: What are the alternatives?* Shall we do it your way or my way, or is it better to find a compromise? What would happen if we tried this? If one does not feel too strongly about the situation, he might say, "Let's try it your way and see if it works." Attack the problem instead of each other.

9. *Be concerned about your partner.* Become involved in your partner's life each day. Try to understand better what the other person thinks and feels and needs.

10. *Make major decisions together.* Responsible choice is one avenue to mature growth.

11. *Don't nag.* Both persons may not see a problem in the same light. To nag each other by scolding, complaining, or faultfinding will not make communication or solution any easier. For example, if you have asked your husband three times to take out the garbage, do not ask him a fourth time. It is easier to take it out yourself than to waste energy harping about something that he apparently does not see as important.

12. *Let bygones be bygones.* If you have a difficulty, work out some sort of solution. Then forget the whole thing if you possibly can. Even if you did not find a satisfactory solution, forget it. There is no use bringing up things that happened last year or five years ago just because you are annoyed about something now. Doing so may relieve your feelings for the moment, but it will not help family relations in the future.

13. *Be optimistic.* Solutions can be found for most problems. A problem is already half solved if you face it with the expectation that some sort of solution is possible. If you cannot work out a solution yourself, seek

professional help. Is the minister who married you the kind of person with whom you can talk things over? If your minister cannot help you, he will probably know of someone who can. There are professionally trained marriage counselors in most cities. There are also family service agencies and pastoral counseling centers in many parts of our country where trained counselors can be of assistance. Should you be unable to find a professional counselor, write to the American Association of Marriage Counselors, Inc., 3603 Lemmon Avenue, Dallas, Texas 75219, or to the American Association of Pastoral Counselors, 201 East 19th Street, New York, New York 10003. These organizations will send you the name of an accredited counselor who lives near you. If your problem is a financial one, there may be a person at your bank who is equipped to give you the advice you need.

14. *Express anger in appropriate ways* when the occasion for anger is at hand—not later.

The Need for Understanding

In a great many households a husband has few interests outside his work. Yet when he tries to talk about his work, his wife shows little interest. Because his mind is on his work, he does not get very excited about his wife's daily schedule.

When Peggy and Joe were married, they loved each other intensely. Joe enjoyed football very much. He had been on the team in high school, where Peggy had admired his ability as a player although she did not care very much for the game. After they were married Joe still liked to go to the high school football games. Peggy went a few times, but she was bored because Joe was not playing. Soon she began to make excuses and stay at home.

The second fall after they were married, Peggy was pregnant. She not only did not want to go to the games, but resented staying at home alone. Joe could not understand why she did not want to go. They argued about this until it became a major issue. Neither seemed able to really understand how the other felt about it. And they may have been quite confused about their emotions.

Peggy, being pregnant, may have been having feelings of isolation or anxiety about her appearance. She may have felt that her husband preferred his old friends. Possibly Joe wondered if he was now appreciated as much by his wife as when he was a football hero. Quite likely he did not understand the changes taking place in Peggy's physical and emotional life. Neither seemed able to talk about their problems without feeling mistreated.

During the winter months Joe began taking Peggy out more frequently to do some of the things she was interested in, and they seemed to get along better. As they became more able to talk over the difficulty they had faced in the fall, they began to understand each other's feelings a little better. They agreed that if they could get a sitter Peggy would occasionally go to the games the following fall and try to understand football a little better. But they would also go to a movie together occasionally. The important thing was that each learned to understand better some of the basic needs and feelings of the other. Because they were able to discuss their difficulties frankly, they could work out a compromise.

You are certain to have some tensions and conflicts to resolve in your marriage. Try to work at solutions calmly and peacefully, accepting the fact that there will be differences of opinion but that most differences can be settled if you work them through responsibly. Problems grow because they are not recognized as problems, or because persons either push them aside and do not try to find a solution or they do not try to understand each other's feelings.

Work on Solutions

Religious faith may be a source of strength when difficulties arise, but it may also be used as a club to hold over a partner's head. "Never let the sun set upon your wrath" is an ancient proverb that points to an important truth: problems which annoy or anger persons should be settled as soon as possible. If no effort is made to eliminate an annoyance, it can fester and grow into a major difficulty. If no solution is worked out for a problem, tension may increase and one person may withdraw, hurt and discouraged.

One value in praying together each night is that barriers between you can be removed before God. Confess to each other unkind deeds or imagined difficulties. Turn to God for forgiveness, for insight, and for strength to handle the difficulties. Some problems cannot be solved immediately, but it will help to know that both of you are trying.

Often the apparently insignificant things can disrupt a marriage. Arguments about finances, friends, recreation, sharing of work, in-laws, discipline of the children, the use of time—almost any aspect of living can be a source of disagreement and argument. What may start out as a minor difficulty may blow up into a storm if a solution is not found.

Early diagnosis of difficulties is important, but direct criticism of each other usually raises defenses rather than solving a problem. If you are sensitive to each other's feelings, you will be able to recognize when conversation is drawing you together or when arguments are driving you apart. When the tone of voice indicates hostility instead of love, accept this as a danger signal and try to discover the cause.

Suffering in silence is rarely a solution and can be damaging to your relationship. But one person must not be left to do all the talking. Unless both of you can share your feelings—either calmly or heatedly—in discussing a problem, it will probably grow. At times, however, your partner may feel deeply hurt about something and it may be best to postpone decisions until you have cooled off a bit, but solutions should not be postponed too long. Continued complaining or nagging may result if you do not promptly and frankly face up to the situation.

Skill in dealing with discord will come if you reflect on your experiences and learn from them. It may be difficult, however, to find the true reason for tensions. Minor frictions may be only symbols of more serious problems. For example, a husband may complain about slight differences of opinion when he really means that he is disappointed because he came to marriage expecting to find complete harmony—no disagreements at all.

He is thrown off balance upon discovering that two married persons do not always think alike.

If such difficulties are drawn out into the open, the process of solving the conflict may actually strengthen a marriage. Doing this may help you redefine your situation and find out just where you are.

When people say, "We have been married fifty years and never had a quarrel," do not believe them. They are idealizing their marriage. What they may mean is that they met their problems in the early days of marriage and developed problem-solving techniques that have allowed them to live together with a minimum of friction. Now they have forgotten that they ever had any difficulties. Or what may have happened is that one person has submitted to domination by the other and they like it that way.

When two people who are used to making their own decisions and living their own lives are suddenly brought together in the intimacies of marriage, it is not surprising that some difficulties arise. If these are handled constructively, the joy of reconciliation will follow, greater maturity will come, and love will be strengthened. Experiences in responsible problem-solving help you grow in confidence that you can face and solve any difficulties that may arise in the future.

Marriage is a shared experience. If one partner is always thinking of his own rights and privileges, he may become so self-centered that he forgets he has responsibilities to others. Marriage is most successful when couples are realistic about mutual tasks to be accomplished and are more concerned about the happiness of their mates than themselves.

Each partner contributes something to a marriage. But each has a personal life to live as well. It should not be necessary to impoverish the life of one to enrich the life of the other. There may be times when one will sacrifice for the benefit of the other, but one person should not make all the sacrifices.

Marriage—A Partnership

As has been said before, marriage is more than a legal contract, more than vows spoken in the presence of God. Marriage is your declared intention before God and the community to live together and, possibly, to rear a family. "For better, for worse" means that you will accept the problems of marriage as well as the privileges. Success in marriage cannot be achieved alone. It calls for a partnership.

In a business partnership each contributes what he has in the way of skill, capital, brains, strength, and experience. Likewise in marriage two people bring to the union their backgrounds, strengths, and abilities. Combining these into a successful partnership, or marriage, requires a willingness to work together and a determination to make a success of the venture. Together you can attain happiness that is not possible if only one person works at the job. Love responds to love and grows best when both husband and wife are concerned about its nurture.

Jealousy is the green-eyed monster that may raise its ugly head in marriage unless you have faith and trust in each other. Fidelity is more than a goal—it is a must. Of course, you renounced all previous love affairs when you became engaged, but you cannot avoid all your former friends. There is usually no reason why you cannot continue to be friends with those you have known in the past as long as it is perfectly clear that your new relationship will not go beyond friendship. If this proves to be difficult, it may be wise to terminate such friendships.

Sometimes old jealousies carry over into a marriage or new ones may arise. It is wise to make every effort not to offend at this point or to give cause for jealousy. Some have tried to cure flagging love in marriage by encouraging jealousy. But once unleashed, jealousy threatens love. It is not a sign of love, but a reflection of immaturity and insecurity in the love relationship. If either of you should have a deep-seated feeling of insecurity, and if jealousy continues after your wedding, you may need to consult with your pastor or a marriage counselor.

Compatibility in Marriage

We hear a great deal of talk these days about the breakdown of marriage because of incompatibility. This simply means "We did not get along together." In some states this is sufficient grounds for divorce.

Often incompatibility is the result of unrealistically high romantic expectations, but there may be some deep and basic reasons why you cannot get along together. Usually if these reasons are discovered, analyzed, and worked through, incompatibility may be avoided and grounds for compatibility discovered and developed.

In every marriage there are times when two people disagree or when they get on each other's nerves. But this is not sufficient grounds for giving up the marriage. Rather, such instances indicate that more attention needs to be given to the marriage relationship.

Faith in each other and in God will help you over the rough places. Weathering the storms together can strengthen a growing marriage. If the going becomes too rough, however, do not hesitate to seek help.

Please read this chapter again after you have been married six or eight months.

CHAPTER IV

Sex in Marriage

This chapter may seem elementary to some readers. It is simply written and included here to give those who have little background or understanding of sexuality and the sexual act some basic knowledge for their marriage relationship. For others, it may be helpful as a review.

Sexuality involves all of life. From the time a child becomes aware of the differences of voice and attitude of his mother and father, he is conscious of sex. In the past we have cultivated sexual difference by dressing baby boys in blue and baby girls in pink; however, this is not so common today. As a child grows older, he begins to realize that certain behavior seems to be associated with maleness or femaleness.

During the teen years physical changes in the body emphasize that a girl or boy is developing as a sexual being. While interest in each other as persons of the opposite sex may not be noticeable in the early teens, suddenly a girl discovers boys, and a little later a boy discovers that it is nice to be near a girl and to hold her hand. One night when he takes her home after a date, he kisses her. If she responds, they may both be a little frightened.

Normally a kiss deepens their relationship, heightens interest in each other, and becomes a bond that ties them together. The relationship may grow and develop into a mature love; however, it is not unusual for a young person to feel that he is in love a number of times. The experience of dating, going steady, falling in and out of love, is all a part of the maturing process. Marriage, however, is such an intimate relationship that it should not be entered into until you are prepared to fully commit yourself. In a good marriage intimacy is much more than physical. It is a sharing of one's whole life with another person.

Someone has said that the toothbrush is the last outpost of privacy. In marriage you share practically everything else—your hopes, your dreams, your money, your recreation, your work.

Physical Attraction

During courtship you have found joy in being together and in sharing physical caresses. Probably there were times when you wished you could go further and complete your sexual union but felt this should be reserved for marriage. Some couples have not waited and have sought release in sexual intercourse, but this is not quite the same as it is after marriage, when intercourse is approved and expected.

The desire for sexual union is perfectly normal, however, and should never be considered wrong and sinful.

71

Sexual relationship is a union of two personalities, a physical expression of self-giving love. Even though we may not completely understand it, it can unite two persons in love and trust as nothing else can do.

Physical love as well as spiritual love ought to grow during your married life so that a year from now, ten years from now, even thirty years from now, you will enjoy being near each other. You may not receive the same electric sparks as when you first held hands, but you will come to know a deep, abiding sense of security and strength. Often just a touch of the hand or a look will say, "I need you," or, "I am glad we have each other," or, "I love you now as always." Such experiences may become as thrilling, as satisfactory, as the exciting experiences of courtship.

Sex Is God-given

If, in childhood, you were taught that sex is dirty and unmentionable, you may have difficulty in finding satisfaction in marital sex relations. Sexual inhibitions in the early days of childhood may have caused you to think of sex only in terms of guilt and shame, instead of recognizing that this is a God-given drive to be accepted and used wisely, as are other God-given hungers.

Sexual desire is normal and natural. In earlier generations it was often considered unladylike for a woman to have any desire for sexual intercourse. It was considered proper only for men to have sexual desire, and women were to "submit" merely because it was their duty. Recent studies and experience over the years indicate, however, that while the feelings of men and women are different, both can find a great joy in the sex act and, in marriage, both should feel free to express their desires.

Understanding Sex

If we understand sex as a part of God's total creation, it may help us in achieving sexual harmony in marriage. Sex is a part of his divine plan. Christian faith affirms sex and calls for the highest expression of sex relations within the covenant relationship of marriage.

Generally the male is more easily aroused sexually than the female. A kiss, the touch of a hand, seeing his wife get ready for bed, or even thinking about his wife may cause a man to respond sexually. A woman may become interested sexually through gentle caresses, kisses, and fond words until she is fully ready for intercourse. If she is tired, she may not be aroused at all and may not be very affectionate. Love play, kissing, fondling, speaking words of endearment contribute to the intensity of sexual feelings and are therefore important in preparation for intercourse in marriage.

Psychological readiness for the love act is also important. Conflicts over money or religion, jealousy, or even the discipline of the children may have an adverse effect on sexual desire. For this reason, an inadequate sex adjustment is often a symptom of disagreement in some other phase of married life. Couples who are well adjusted in most aspects of family living generally find little difficulty in coming together in sexual union.

Nevertheless, sexual adjustment requires skill and practice, just as does solving money problems, or becoming a good cook, or accepting each other's differences. Willingness to try to please each other and recognition of sex as a God-given aspect of marriage lead to greater happiness.

No one can lay down rules for your sexual relationship, for no two persons respond to each other in exactly the same way. There is no norm. Each couple will have to work out an adjustment that is satisfactory to them alone. You will need patience and concern for each other in order to achieve mutual happiness. It goes without saying that sexual intercourse or the withholding of it should never be used as a weapon.

The following illustrations are included for the benefit of some who need to know more about human anatomy.

The sex act in marriage is more than a reproductive

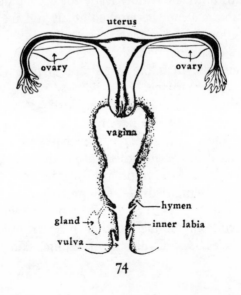

function. It also provides a sense of unity and well-being between a man and a woman. Only human beings experience sex for both procreation and pleasure.

When a man is aroused sexually, blood flows more rapidly through the penis and it becomes enlarged and firm. Sensitive nerve endings in the penis make it one of the centers of sexual pleasure for a man. Underneath the penis hangs a bag, or scrotum, in which are two testicles, about the size of walnuts. These produce spermatozoa which fertilize the egg or ovum in the woman. They also produce the male sex hormones which affect other bodily functions in the male, such as the change of voice and the growth of hair at puberty. Spermatozoa, or sperm cells, are produced in large quan-

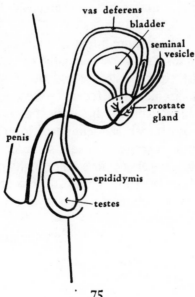

tities. These are transmitted in the semen, the white fluid which flows from the penis at the climax of intercourse. The sperm cells have little tails which make it possible for them to move rapidly up through the woman's vagina into the pear-shaped organ called the uterus, and thence into the Fallopian tubes.

The egg, or ovum, develops in the ovary of the woman. At the time of ovulation, about fourteen days before menstruation begins, the egg leaves the ovary and travels down into the Fallopian tubes toward the uterus, about a two-day journey. If sperm and egg meet there and the sperm penetrates the egg, conception takes place, the fertilized egg becomes implanted in the wall of the uterus, and pregnancy develops. The menstrual flow is altered to maintain the pregnancy. Otherwise, the egg and lining of the uterus are discharged at the time of menstruation.

Some persons have more interest and pleasure in sexual relations than others. It is generally easy for men to achieve a satisfactory climax, or orgasm. Most men have a climax and ejaculation after a few seconds to a few minutes. In most women, however, orgasm may take longer and is not nearly as definite or localized as it is for a man. Some may experience a sense of elation and well-being and never achieve the high moment of ecstacy known as orgasm. About 70 percent of women achieve orgasm sometime during the first year of marriage.[1]

It should be remembered that the popular concepts of

[1] A. C. Kinsey, W. B. Pomeroy, C. E. Martin, and P. H. Gelbad, *Sexual Behavior in the Human Female* (W. B. Sanders, 1953).

sexual pleasure that are portrayed in movies and fiction are often misleading. A wife need not feel abnormal if she does not reach orgasm every time during intercourse. Many women are happy and quite satisfied with a general sense of well-being rather than an erotic climax. Each wife has her own unique way of experiencing the moment of intimacy, and there is no way of pre-planning or predicting what it will be.

Capacity for orgasm seems to increase with age and experience. When too much stress is placed upon the importance of achieving mutual orgasm, however, a couple's love-making may be artificial, frustrating, and strained. If, through intercourse, you are able to achieve a sense of well-being and oneness, this should be sufficient.

Expect that there will be occasions which are much more satisfactory than others. True love-making entails consideration for the other partner as the primary concern, with personal gratification secondary. Achieving sexual pleasure is an art requiring love, knowledge, and practice.

The apostle Paul in his letter to the Corinthians gave this advice: "The husband should give to his wife her conjugal rights, and likewise the wife to her husband. For the wife does not rule over her own body, but the husband does; likewise the husband does not rule over his own body, but the wife does. Do not refuse one another except perhaps by agreement for a season, that you may devote yourselves to prayer; but then come together again" (I Corinthians 7:3-5). Mutuality may be the key to a happy adjustment.

Full sexual satisfaction is not usually achieved the first night of marriage. Many do not find sexual intercourse nearly as satisfactory as they expected it to be. It may take months, or even years, for a couple to achieve the highest degree of sexual fulfillment of which they are capable.

In both men and women, fatigue is often a factor in sexual response. A person who is physically tired may prefer sleep to love-making. This may be understandable some of the time, but not all of the time. If it happens too often, it may indicate that one of you is working too hard, is in need of a physical check-up, or may be using sleep as resistance to sex.

Sometimes couples work too hard for the good of their marriage. Making love is a twenty-four-hour-a-day task and does not begin just when the bedroom door is closed. The little things of life are very meaningful in the love relationship, and the attitude of two married people toward each other during the day will have a great deal to do with the preparation for adequate physical relationship when they go to bed.

Talk About It

How can you please each other if you do not know what each desires? Many couples have great difficulty discussing their sexual feelings. They keep quiet about feelings, their likes and dislikes in the area of sexual relations. Often one unknowingly goes on offending the other. Many a man would like his wife to be more responsive, but has never talked with her about it.

Some couples tend to shut off their feelings from each other and become withdrawn. Actually they should become more and more open with each other as the months go by. For example, one person may want to experiment with various positions in intercourse or with manipulation of the sex organs, but never lets the other know. Or, one may feel that the other is oversexed or a pervert if he or she wants to experiment with sex. Certainly each person's aesthetic values must be considered, but sex practices are right or wrong for you depending upon your own desires and understanding of sexual relationships. Freedom in talking about sexual relations may save you from years of unhappiness.

Try to understand your mate's needs and desires. The sex relationship is more than providing for each other's rights and privileges. It is a joy to be shared. You will work out your own techniques for letting each other know when intercourse is desired. Some men find it difficult to adjust their sexual climax to a wife's readiness for intercourse. It is not at all unusual on the honeymoon for a man to have a premature ejaculation and to feel very embarrassed about his inability to complete the sexual act. Normally this will be overcome with practice.

Some persons seem to desire sexual relations much more frequently than others. After the honeymoon you may settle down to a pattern of two or three times a week, but you cannot make love by the calendar. One may desire to be together more than the other, and it will be necessary to work out times that are mutually desirable. Or it may be necessary for one to make a special effort to be interested for the sake of the other.

If you are very tired, you may not desire intercourse for several days. But do not feel that either of you is not in love just because intercourse is not desired as frequently as during the honeymoon.

Sexual satisfaction is more likely to be achieved when other conditions are just right. After a happy day or a pleasant evening in each other's company you may want to be close together. Or if you have been very tired during the day, the morning may be a happier time for intercourse.

Because of the overemphasis on sex in our culture today, or because of differences in background, you may not find the thrill in intercourse which you expected or which your reading has indicated you ought to find. Be patient. Seek satisfaction in other aspects of living as well. Through your work, your hobbies, your recreation and other common interests, you can find a rich union of your personalities. As you draw closer together through a deeper sharing of your hopes and your activities, you will find a deeper meaning and richer enjoyment in the sexual union. Keep looking for those activities that lead to unity and understanding rather than concentrating on the differences in your lives.

A premarital examination by a physician is recommended for both the man and the woman, not only to discover possible disease but to determine whether or not normal sexual relations are possible. For example, the doctor may cut the hymen (the fold of mucous membrane partly closing the opening of the woman's vagina) if it is unusually tough, or he may make other recommendations for the fuller enjoyment of intercourse.

Fear of pregnancy may affect sexual response. Even though you may want children sometime in the future, you will be most likely to give yourself joyously to each other in marriage if adequate precaution has been taken to avoid pregnancy. If requested, your physician will advise you regarding the best method for you to use.

In case one person is a Roman Catholic, or belongs to some other religious group that does not approve the use of modern methods of birth control, the partner will want to respect his feelings. Full understanding and appreciation of the philosophy of the church is essential. The United Methodist position is stated as follows: "We believe that responsible family planning, practiced in Christian conscience, fulfills the will of God. The present population problems call for a continuing responsible attitude toward family planning." (From *The Book of Resolutions of The United Methodist Church* 1968, pp. 89-90.)

Planning for Children

Many couples want children. Even with the wide knowledge of birth control methods, the average American couple has three or four children. Typically the children have come quite early in marriage and fairly close together. Some couples, however, do not desire children immediately. They feel it would be better to wait two or three years until they feel more secure about their marriage and have saved a little money. Such planning is recommended by many authorities. This does not mean, of course, that those who have their children earlier do not love them. Even children whose births

81

were not planned may be a source of great joy and genuine love.

Although some couples want a baby for very inadequate reasons, such as to patch up an already failing marriage, the majority want children because they feel life is not complete without them. Providing for a new life may draw a couple closer together, but if they are not ready to assume this responsibility, the advent of a child may drive them farther apart.

Proper spacing of children is recommended both for the health of the mother and to allow parents greater ease in caring for their children. In a study of child-rearing patterns conducted a few years ago, 81 percent of those who were about to have their first child were pleased or completely delighted to know that the wife was pregnant. But the situation was different for succeeding children. If the next child came within twenty-one months or less, only 9 percent were pleased and 68 percent had mixed feelings or were displeased. If the second child was not born for thirty-two months or more, two thirds of the parents were delighted to welcome the child while only a few were displeased. The greater distance between children up to a point in time, the happier the mother may be about another pregnancy.[2]

Although methods of planned parenthood are widely discussed today, only brief mention will be made here of the more common methods of conception control. Talk with your doctor about the best method for you, or visit a planned parenthood clinic. Most clinics are also

[2] James A. Peterson, *Education for Marriage* (Scribner's, 1964), p. 336.

concerned about fertility, and the couple facing difficulty in having children can find help there, as well as from the wife's gynecologist.

The Pill

In the United States one of the most widespread methods of controlling conception has been the use of "the pill." This oral contraceptive contains synthetic hormones that prevent the production of eggs in the ovary. The pill is available from drugstores on prescription from a physician and should be taken according to his directions for twenty or twenty-one days out of the month. During the next ten days menstruation takes place normally, after which the dosage is resumed. When the pill is discontinued, normal conception is likely to take place.

The pill is considered a safe and satisfactory method of avoiding conception for most women, but some experience undesirable side effects and they are not able to use it. Because of certain physical conditions, doctors sometimes will not prescribe pills but will suggest another method of control.

The Diaphragm

Dr. Allen F. Guttenmacher, active leader in the Planned Parenthood movement, recommends for newlyweds either the steroid pill mentioned above or the use of the diaphragm with a spermicidal jelly or cream. Either requires the guidance of a physician.

The diaphragm is a thin rubber membrane inserted into the vagina by the woman so that it covers the end of the cervix and blocks the sperm from entering the womb. The doctor will give instructions regarding the size and placement of the diaphragm and its use.

The Condom

If the husband wishes to control conception, he may be willing to use a rubber condom which may be obtained from any drugstore without prescription. With careful use this has the advantage of being fairly certain, but some couples find it inconvenient and uncomfortable. Friction may be alleviated by the use of a little lubricating jelly sold in drugstores. Some prefer a condom made of animal tissue which has been prelubricated.

The Rhythm Method

Rhythm and abstinence are the only methods recommended by the Roman Catholic Church for controlling conception. The rhythm method is based upon the fact that conception can take place only during a few days of the menstrual cycle. Every menstrual month an ovum (or occasionally two ova) is released from an ovary. This process is called ovulation. Ovulation generally takes place approximately fourteen days before the beginning of the next menstrual period. This means that if a woman's menstrual cycle is regular at twenty-eight days, ovulation can be expected to take place approximately fourteen days after the beginning of the previous menstrual flow. It is possible to predict the onset of ovulation on the basis of a woman's menstrual history, but there are many variables (physical illness, emotional upset, and so forth) which may cause ovulation to take place earlier or later in the menstrual month. Further, the fact that a woman's menstrual cycle has been regular in the past does not mean that it will always be regular.

Since the male sperm remains active for about forty-eight hours, it is necessary for a couple using the rhythm method of birth control to accurately predict ovulation and abstain from sexual union for two or three days before and two or three days after ovulation, if pregnancy is to be avoided.

Since the rhythm method is one of the least effective methods of planned parenthood, it cannot be recommended except in instances of interfaith marriage when conscience will not permit a member of the Roman Catholic Church to use other and more effective methods. A couple using this method of contraception should be aware of the fact that a pregnancy may result.

Intrauterine Contraceptive Device (IUD)

Intrauterine contraceptive devices are among the oldest forms of contraception. It has only been in recent years, however, that they have been developed to the point that they are now among the most widely used and effective methods of birth control. The IUD is a plastic device, shaped as a spiral, bow, loop, or coil, which is inserted into the uterus by a private physician or specially trained personnel of a birth control clinic.

The device may be left in place indefinitely and can easily be removed by a physician when a pregnancy is desired. A medical examination is advisable every six months to make sure that everything is in order.

This method of contraception is not usually recommended until after the birth of the first child. Brides who have not had a previous pregnancy will need to consider another method of contraception at the start of their marriage.

Other Methods

A variety of jellies, foams, and creams have been developed which are now fairly effective, but as a rule not as effective as the methods discussed above. A douche alone may help avoid some pregnancies but is not a sufficiently effective method to be recommended.

Coitus interruptus, or withdrawal of the penis before ejaculation, is probably the oldest method of birth control, but this is not entirely dependable, for occasionally some sperm will get into the vagina before withdrawal. Much of the satisfaction of intercourse is also lost for both husband and wife.

Couples who desire a more thorough discussion of birth control are referred to the sources listed in the bibliography on page 126.

If You Cannot Have Children

In about one out of ten marriages either the husband or wife is infertile, or sterile, and it is not possible for them to have children. Planned parenthood fertility clinics or gynecologists may be able to help some, but not all, of these couples. It is not necessary for a couple who cannot have children to remain childless, however. Many parentless children of all ages need love and a good home.

If you decide to adopt a child, be sure to apply only to a reliable licensed agency. Much heartbreak has resulted from dealing with a blackmarket or unauthorized agency. A couple seeking a child for adoption should welcome the interviews and investigations made by the agency. That same agency will be just as careful to screen the child's background so that the adopting parents receive a healthy, normal child. The agency will also work out any legal questions involved. There may be some delay, but the baby will be worth waiting for. Usually there is a probation period before final papers are signed.

In Conclusion

Sexual relationships bridge the isolation and apartness of two individuals. The union achieved is often an expression of the deepest feelings of concern, pride in oneself and the other, and desire to see the other find fulfillment. God, therefore, is in the relationship. As Jesus saw it, the two become one flesh in this expression of marriage. When a husband and wife come together in the sex act, it is a holy moment of deep personal communion.

CHAPTER V

Marriage—An Achievement

A good marriage does not just happen. It is dependent on the determination and willingness of both persons to work for a sound and lasting relationship. Couples who take their marriage for granted are much more likely to drift apart than to drift together.

The Honeymoon Is a Beginning

Dr. C. Stedman Glisson, Jr., a physician vitally interested in preparation for marriage, says: "Courtship is a period of salesmanship when the best foot in put forward. No salesman emphasizes the product's weaknesses. The honeymoon resembles the shakedown cruise for any ship that must be evaluated. Although built to the best and most exacting specifications, the way she handles must be evaluated under varying circumstances, and allowances made for different routines worked out to correct flaws."

The purpose of the honeymoon is to allow a little time for the bride and groom to get away from their families and friends and begin to adjust to each other before becoming involved in the routines of daily living. Some weddings are preceded by a number of parties and activities, and both bride and groom may be exhausted. They need to get away by themselves for a few quiet days together.

It is best not to tell anyone where you are going, or you may be bothered by pranksters, visitors, or telephone calls. One person in each family, however, should know where to reach you in case of an emergency, and parents will appreciate a telephone call to know that you have arrived safely at your destination.

It is usually best not to go too far away and to avoid traveling every day. Make your reservations, at least for the first night or two, well in advance so that you will be sure of a place to stay. There is considerable strain involved in visiting relatives, so it is best to stay at a motel, hotel, or resort where you can be completely alone.

Planning for the honeymoon should be done together, and arrangements should be acceptable to both of you. Unless you are very enthusiastic campers, the probability is that you will not want to go on a camping trip. Some couples, however, do like camping and have had enough experience beforehand to know that they will really enjoy being with each other in some rough situations.

You do not need to plan a long honeymoon. The short, inexpensive trip with pleasant accommodations will probably be a happier experience than a longer trip for which you spend too much money. A honeymoon is worth some sacrifices, but you do not want to return to your new home completely broke.

A Feeling of Oneness

The union of two persons comes from the ability to work together, play together, solve problems together, and face tragedy together. Learning how to do this takes time. Many couples are disappointed because a few days of honeymooning do not result in a complete feeling of unity. In fact, this time together may merely reveal some of your differences which you had not recognized before. If so, don't panic. Most obstacles, differences, or problems can be worked through.

But if the difficulty should be too much for you to handle alone, do not hesitate to call on your minister or a marriage counselor for help. He is as near as your telephone. You can probably work out most adjustments by yourselves; however, if you have done your best and find you are getting nowhere fast, or if you see that your problem is getting worse instead of better, ask for help.

Separations

You have decided to get married because you want to be together, but separations are certain to come. For example, military service may separate you for a while. If so, try to be together as much as possible. Military bases usually do not provide very comfortable living quarters, but if it is possible to have a room or apartment near the base, consider putting up with some inconvenience rather than being separated. These are years when you will be growing together, and you will need every opportunity to become better acquainted.

There may be periods of homesickness, especially for a wife, if she has not been accustomed to being away from home. You may feel a desire to run home with your problems. An occasional visit may be helpful, but remember that after marriage the primary relationship in your life, for both husband and wife, is to each other. Make your own decisions and make them together.

Your Home—A Christian Home

You have come to your minister asking his guidance as you enter into a Christian marriage. In establishing your new home, do not lose sight of the fact that yours is a Christian marriage, and endeavor to make your home one that is truly Christian.

When you have your first meal together, you will wish to thank God for the opportunity to establish a Christian home. Use a brief prayer such as the following:

Our heavenly Father, we thank you for our love for each other and for our new home. As we begin our life together, we dedicate our home to Christian living. Bless us, we pray, that our home may be a place of peace and harmony. May we try at all times to show love and respect for each other, in keeping with the way Jesus taught us to live. Amen.

When you are ready and buy a home, you may wish to invite your minister to help you dedicate it. The United Methodist Church has a special ritual for the dedication of a home. (See "An Office for the Blessing of a Dwelling" in *The Book of Worship for Church and*

Home.) Your friends and relatives will want to join you in this act of dedication.

What Is a Christian Family?

The United Methodist Church has stated that six essential characteristics distinguish a Christian family.

(1) In a Christian family, members respond in faith and love to God as revealed in Jesus Christ. They face the everyday experiences, as well as the great joys and tragedies of life, within the context of their faith in God. A Christian family endeavors to bring every member into a living relationship to God and a total commitment to Jesus Christ.

(2) In a Christian family, marriage is seen as a covenant relationship, parenthood as a Christian vocation, and all human relationships as sacred. Thus, family members function faithfully in marriage, parenthood, and family responsibilities, according to their understanding of God's will for them.

(3) Not only may members of a Christian family live in a common household and share a family name, but they are also bound together as Christians and are an integral part of the church. The nature and mission of the Christian community come to expression in and through the family as well as in the congregation.

(4) A Christian family member endeavors to live in the spirit of Christ in every relationship—with himself, with other persons, with the world, with history, and with God. Especially in the relationships of husband and wife, mother and father, son and daughter, brother and

sister, he strives to grow in expressing God's unconditional love—sacrificing, forgiving, sustaining.

(5) A Christian family, while performing certain functions within society, is at the same time an expression of the kingdom of God. With a sense of discipleship, members of a Christian family work with God to accomplish his purposes in the world.

(6) A Christian family creates, sustains, and transmits a culture of Christian traditions and values. This culture finds expression in a variety of ritual practices, religious symbols, and a life style reflecting the spirit of Christ in the day-to-day experiences of life.[1]

Any shared interest encourages unity in marriage, but to be able to share the sacred experiences of life, such as prayer, attending church, partaking of the Holy Communion, and the dedication of children in baptism, binds persons together as nothing else can. And in such experiences even those who differ in religious beliefs may find points at which they can agree.

Commitment to Christian ideals helps a person determine his goals. If husband and wife have similar ideals and purposes rooted in their Christian beliefs, there is likely to be harmony in their marriage. Their faith will give them confidence and purpose in daily living.

It is easier to establish the intimate relationships of worship in the early days of marriage than later, and special devotional materials have been written for possible use during the first month of marriage. Recommended resources are also listed on page 126. Your re-

[1] From *The Book of Resolutions of The United Methodist Church,* 1968, pp. 89-90.

ligious practices can be a decisive force in your marriage and may bring you closer together than you have ever been before as, together, you seek the presence of God.

Will there be Christian symbols in your home? Symbols are visible representations of an ideal or attribute. They are valuable in calling attention to that for which they stand. The Bible, the cross, a candle, a religious picture, or a shelf of devotional books reminds you and others of your Christian commitment.

You will want your children to grow up with a strong Christian faith. The time to prepare for nurturing the religious growth of your children is before they are born. As you increase your knowledge of the Bible and learn how to use worship resources creatively, you will be preparing to guide them in their worship experiences.

Have you talked about your plans for worship together? If you find this difficult, talk to your minister about it.

Children in a Christian Home

When children come into your home, either by birth or adoption, you will want them to be baptized as members of the family of God. In this sacramental act parents agree, with the help of the church, to guide their children into a Christian style of life. Baptism enrolls the child as a preparatory member of the church, and when he is old enough he becomes a full member by assuming the vows himself in a service of confirmation.

Sharing your life with a child brings additional responsibilities and duties. The mother, of course, will carry the greater responsibility for the everyday care of children, but children need fathers too. Neither parent can take the place of the other. While it may be nice to have the children in bed when Father comes home so that parents can have some time together, children also need time to be with their father for mutual expression of love and affection. What a father gives to a child emotionally is as important as what he gives financially.

Before your children arrive, you will want to learn all you can about the emotional needs of children and how to satisfy these needs. You may have had some courses in child psychology and child development in college, but you will need to continue studying and reading in this area. Check to see what courses are currently available through your church or community agencies. Your community or church library may have books and magazines that also will be helpful.

The Christian Home, a monthly magazine for parents, published by The United Methodist Church, contains articles on child care and Christian teaching in the home. Special articles each month deal with such problems as finances, jealousy, temper tantrums, disobedience, fears, stealing, sex education, and discipline. Some churches subscribe to this magazine for all parents of young children, but it is also available for individual subscription.

Keep Romance in Your Marriage

It was suggested earlier in this book that as you enter marriage, you will want to give up some of your romantic notions about marriage. You will discover that marriage is more than holding hands, going out together, and so forth, but such things can add much to the enjoyment of each other's company. It is important to make time each day for love and attention to each other.

After your children arrive, you probably will not have as much time for each other as formerly, but it is essential that you find some time to do things together. Couples should learn to share books, magazines, the daily newspaper, and news commentators' views so that both may keep up to date. Most churches provide nursery care so you can attend church and Sunday school together.

Many couples write into their budget an amount for a baby sitter one night a week so they can go out together. If you cannot afford a baby sitter, you may be able to work out an exchange with another couple. Perhaps you cannot do all the things you enjoyed doing before the baby arrived, but do not neglect your hobbies and interests, for you will want to return to some of them more actively after the first years of child care have passed. Whatever your situation, save as much time as you can for each other. Often a brief time away from children strengthens your love for each other and increases your appreciation of your home and family.

Opportunities for Growth in the Church

Most churches now have church school classes or other groups for young couples which will strengthen your religious life. If your church does not have some kind of meeting or study group for young couples, either before or after they have children, talk with your minister about the possibility of starting one. Such a group will provide an opportunity to study family relationships. Church libraries are a source of inspiration and help, too, providing books on marriage, child care, and Bible study.

You will teach your children primarily by example. As you grow in your own Christian life, your home becomes a Christian home. In the Christian home, your family will develop Christian ideals, attitudes, and relationships. Children learn to believe in a loving God as they see love in their parents. If they can trust their parents, it will not be difficult for them to trust God. Parents' speech and behavior, of course, must be in keeping with their profession of faith. Church attendance and support of the church teaches children that their parents believe in the church.

Christian Living Requires Action

As Christians, you will not be self-centered, interested only in your own home and family. You will be concerned about the problems of the community in which you live and about the needs of persons throughout the world. You will accept responsibility for working in your church and your community. Through church and community activities you will attempt to minister to persons and find ways of easing the tensions of modern living. You will be mindful not only of your own family but also of the other families in your community, as well as in Korea, India, the Philippines, and elsewhere.

Christianity is an everyday style of life. The bonds of marriage will be strengthened as, together, you witness for Christ in your community and the world.

97

CHAPTER VI

Wedding Plans

"I have always wanted a church wedding," she said, "but Donald doesn't want a big wedding."

"I am glad you talked it over," replied the minister. "How does your family feel about it?"

"Mother would like me to have a big wedding, but I only want a couple of bridesmaids."

"You don't have to have a large wedding to have it in the church," said the minister. "We would be happy to marry you before the altar even if only you and Donald and two witnesses were present. But of course you can invite as many others as you wish."

"Will the service be any longer in the church sanctuary than the chapel?"

"No, it will be the same service whether in the church or anywhere else."

Most ministers feel that there is no more sacred place to unite two people in marriage than before the altar of the church or chapel. The altar symbolizes dedication.

It is not necessary to spend a great deal of money on a church wedding, however. Decorations can be very simple, or you may decide not to have any at all. If you feel uncomfortable about the walk down the aisle and a church full of people, simply invite a few friends and come into the church informally with the minister to stand before the altar.

A Home or Church Wedding?

Even if you decide to have no flowers and only the witnesses required by law, your minister will still prefer to take you into the church sanctuary or chapel for the service. Legally you may be married in your home or in the church parlor, but a service in the church adds dignity and meaning to the marriage ceremony. You expect to be married only once. Make your wedding a happy memory.

Nearly all ministers object to performing weddings in unusual places such as a boat or plane. The purpose of stunt weddings is to attract the attention of a crowd and sometimes to publicize a commercial product. The minister will not wish to add the blessing of the church to this kind of situation.

Sometimes a home wedding is in keeping with family traditions. When this is the case, a beautiful garden or a room arranged with flowers to represent the altar and with Christian symbols, such as a cross or candles, to show that this is a religious occasion may be the setting for a wedding.

Whom to Invite

Your invitation list will begin with your immediate families. Mothers and fathers have been looking forward to this event for a long time, and if no one else is invited, they should be included. Even though you may not have been on intimate terms with some members of your family, it will help family relationships if you invite them to your wedding. When you exclude relatives, you are denying them the opportunity to be together for a happy and sacred family occasion. Taking your vows before your family, friends, and fellow members of the church will strengthen your marriage. You feel that you will always have the prayers and best wishes of your loved ones with you, and witnessing your marriage should strengthen the determination of those who are present to keep their own vows.

Both the bride's family and the groom's family usually make up lists of persons who are to be invited. These persons are then invited by the parents of the bride to attend the wedding. If you have been very active in your church, you may wish to place a general invitation to all members of the church in your church bulletin.

If the wedding is to be a small, intimate affair, you may call your friends on the telephone or write an informal note, asking them to be present. People consider it a compliment to be included. If formal invitations are to be sent out, however, tradition dictates that they be mailed three or four weeks in advance.

You may send some people an invitation only to the wedding at the church, but for special friends include a card inviting them to the reception. Or if all those who are invited to the wedding are also invited to the reception, you may indicate on the invitation itself the time and place of the reception.

It is customary to send an invitation to the wedding and reception to the minister and his wife. The minister's wife is not obligated to attend all weddings at the church, however. They do not usually send a gift.

In planning your wedding you may wish to consult books that give detailed information on wedding arrangements and etiquette. These can be found in most public libraries. Several are listed on page 127. You will find that authorities do not always agree and, of course, traditions differ in various parts of the country. Your minister has had a wide experience in helping couples plan their weddings and will be happy to be of assistance to you.

Local Church Customs

There are certain customs and regulations in each locality that should be considered in planning for a wedding. If you choose to be married in your church, you will want your wedding to be in keeping with these traditions and regulations.

For example, in many churches there are rules concerning the decorations. If your florist is accustomed to decorating in a particular church, he will be familiar with these rules, but it is best to check. Removing the pulpit or Communion table, or obstructing the view of the altar, is not considered appropriate in any church. Neither is it appropriate to change a church into a flower garden.

It is customary for the bride's parents to decorate the church and furnish flowers for the attendants. The groom usually pays for the bride's bouquet as well as flowers for the mother of the bride and for his own mother. In most cases the same florist furnishes all the flowers, but the groom can arrange to pay his part of the bill.

Some Churches Have Fixed Charges

There is no charge for weddings in most churches if either the bride or the groom or their families are members of the church. If you are being married in a church other than your own, however, there may be a fee. In some communities it is customary to give the sexton a small gift, depending upon how much extra work you have made for him. In other churches there is a stated fee for the use of the church which includes an adequate sum for the sexton, who must prepare for and clean up after the ceremony. The bride's family takes care of all expenses related to the use of the church. If you have questions, consult the minister.

The regular organist of the church is familiar with the organ and will probably be able to provide the best music for your wedding. There may be a fixed fee for his services. Otherwise a gift of money is customary. If you wish to have a close friend play the organ, check with the church organist to see if this is permitted. Organs are expensive and sometimes temperamental instruments. In some churches regulations have been made regarding their use.

Traditionally it has been appropriate for the groom to give the minister a gift of money. This is not in any sense to pay for his services, for he makes no charge. It is, rather, a token of appreciation. He may accept it or not, as he wishes.

Suitable Music

The music determines the mood for a wedding. Traditionally the bride and attendants entered to the strains of "Lohengrin" and left the atlar to the majestic bars of Mendelssohn's "Wedding March." There has been a trend away from this music in recent years, however. You or the organist may wish to suggest something of a more religious nature. Much progress has been made in the last fifteen years in the selection of suitable music for weddings. A good organist can guide you in selecting appropriate music.

The organist should be in his place thirty minutes ahead of time, and any special solos, either vocal or instrumental, should come in advance of the hour set for the wedding. Many ministers feel there should be no music during the ceremony, especially during the prayers. Others permit the organist to play very softly.

Photographs

You probably will want pictures of your wedding, but you do not want the solemnity of the service marred by photographers running up and down the aisles and the popping of flash bulbs. The Professional Photographers of America has prepared a "professional code of ethics for church weddings" which recognizes that a wedding is a service of divine worship and should not be interrupted

103

by picture-taking. Pictures should be taken before or after the ceremony unless the photographer can operate from the rear of the church without using flash bulbs.

Check with your minister regarding customs in your church. If you want pictures of the ceremony before the altar, the minister will be happy to have you come back into the church after the service and pose for them. Why not wait until after the reception for pictures, so as not to delay those waiting to greet you?

The bride's family usually pays for pictures in the bride's book, but if they cannot afford this expense, the couple may offer to pay for the pictures. If other friends or relatives would like to have pictures, they can order from the photographer.

The Rehearsal

If you are planning a church wedding for more than a few intimate friends, it is essential to have a rehearsal. At the time you make arrangements for your wedding, set the date for the rehearsal with the minister and the organist.

The rehearsal is usually held the night before or the morning of the wedding. It will have to be at a time when all or most of the attendants can be present, for it is important for each person to know exactly what to do.

If the rehearsal is held in the evening, it is customary to have a supper for the wedding party either before or after the rehearsal. This is often given by the parents of the groom or by the best man, but if no one else offers, the bride's family makes the arrangements. The idea that the groom should go out for a bachelor supper to celebrate his last night of freedom has been relegated to the ash heap because a different view of marriage prevails today.

It is a gracious gesture to invite your minister and his wife to the rehearsal supper, although he may not be able to attend because of his heavy schedule. As this is a United Methodist wedding, it would not be in good taste to serve alcoholic beverages. The United Methodist Church has taken a strong stand against social drinking, and it would be against the tradition of the church to serve alcoholic drinks at any social affair related to your wedding. This is not "expected" in connection with United Methodist weddings.

The Minister in Charge

The wedding is a religious ceremony, and the minister is in charge of both the rehearsal and the ceremony. He has participated in many weddings and may have definite convictions regarding the way they should be conducted. Therefore it is important to go over all details with him before the rehearsal. You may wish to make suggestions, but he is in charge of the service.

Sometimes feelings are hurt because guests and relatives have conflicting ideas regarding the way the couple should stand before the altar or the way the bride and attendants should walk down the aisle. If the bride and groom talk over their plans with the minister in advance, he can make the decisions.

In some communities there is a professional bridal consultant connected with a department store or florist's shop who is available to direct a wedding. If you engage the services of this person, remind him or her to discuss plans with the minister in advance because the minister's decision is final. A consultant can be helpful in arranging dresses and getting people ready on time at the back of the church, but the minister is in charge of the ceremony before the altar.

Traditions Vary

The United Methodist Church has an official ritual, approved by the General Conference, which should be followed as closely as possible. Study it carefully so that you understand the meaning of the vows you are about to take. (See Chapter I and pages 120-25.)

Your minister may wish to add a selection of Scripture or an extemporaneous prayer, but most ministers follow the official ritual.

Traditionally the groom does not see the bride in her wedding gown until she comes down the aisle. This custom goes back to the days of arranged marriages when the groom did not see the bride until the day of the wedding.

The custom of giving the bride away also has its origin in the ancient custom of giving the bride from one family to another. Our term *wedlock* comes from Anglo-Saxon words *wed*, meaning to pledge, and *lac*, meaning a gift. The terms referred to the pledge of the groom that he would marry the bride and to the dowry given by the bride's father.

Giving wedding gifts is an old American custom. In pioneer days when a couple married, they usually built a cabin and moved from their parents' home into a new home. Money was scarce and stores were far away. Parents and friends gave gifts to help the newlyweds furnish their new home. In recent years some brides and grooms exchange gifts and present gifts to their attendants.

The Ushers

Ushers should be at the church an hour before time for the service to begin. They seat the bride's family and friends on the left side of the church, facing the altar, and the groom's family and friends on the right side. If the groom is from out of town, and has few friends present, it is better to balance the seating.

The usher offers his right arm to a lady and takes her to the pew. If she is accompanied by a man, he follows after them. If the pew is on his right side, the usher turns and waits for both to move into the pew before he returns to the head of the aisle to meet the next guest. If the pew is on the left side, the usher stops at the pew and the guests pass in front of him into the pew.

Just before the wedding march begins, an usher takes the mother of the bride down the aisle on his right arm, waits for her to cross in front of him and enter the left front seat, leaving the seat next to the aisle for the father. (The mother and father of the groom have been seated earlier in the right front pew.)

Traditionally the mother of the bride sits alone until her husband or a close relative gives away the bride and come to sit with her. If she prefers not to sit alone, another close relative may sit in the pew with her but should be seated much earlier. When there is no center aisle, the bride's family comes down the left aisle and the groom's family comes down the right aisle. Both families sit in the center section if there is room. If a white canvas or other material is to be used to cover the aisle, the ushers (or the sexton) draw it from the front to the back of the aisle just before the bridal party enters.

The Bridal Party

The wedding march should begin promptly at the time set for the wedding. An usher or other designated person gives the signal to the organist that all are ready.

The wedding party comes down the center aisle, if there is one, and returns the same way. If the church has two principal aisles, it is customary to enter by the left aisle, facing the altar, and return by the right aisle.

In some communities there is a tradition that the congregation shall remain seated during the wedding procession, but the Order for the Service of Marriage found in The United Methodist Church's *Book of Worship for Church and Home* states that "the congregation shall stand as the wedding procession begins" (page 28). The congregation will not stand unless the mother of the bride arises, however, and everyone will be seated after the processional if she sits down. Your minister can advise on local customs.

When the wedding march begins, the minister enters first, by a front door. He is followed by the groom and the best man. If all the men wear gloves, the groom removes his right glove and carries it in his left hand. If a double ring ceremony is to be used, he may put his gloves in his pocket or hand them to the best man when the bride hands her flowers to the maid of honor. The groom takes his place just in front of his parents, who are in the front row right, next to the aisle. The best man stops beside him. Both face the aisle.

The ushers come down the aisle first, usually two by two. Since it is difficult for men to use the slow step often used by the women, the organist might set a moderate tempo for all to keep step to as they move to their places.

At one time it was customary for the men to stand on the right and the women on the left before the altar, but it has now become the custom to alternate. When the first two men come down the aisle, one goes to the farthest place on each side, and those who follow do the same. Unless the groom is shorter than the ushers, the tall persons stand in the center and the shorter ones on either side. All face the aisle, watching the bridesmaids and the bride come down the aisle.

Many couples do not have a large number of attendants. But there will be at least a bride and groom and two attendants and possibly the father of the bride. In this case they stand in the same location as indicated on the chart below. If there are more bridesmaids and ushers, an equal number will stand on the right and left respectively.

Bridesmaids and other attendants come down the aisle one at a time in the following order: bridesmaids, matron of honor, maid of honor, flower girl, ring bearer, and bride. It is not necessary to have a matron of honor *and* a maid of honor. Nor is it necessary to have a flower girl or ring bearer. If there is a ring bearer, however, pin the ring or rings carefully to the pillow so that the minister can get them easily.

If there is no ring bearer (only at one in ten church weddings are there children attendants), the best man carries the bride's ring. If two rings are to be used, the maid of honor carries the groom's ring. (The groom buys the wedding ring for the bride, and the bride is expected to pay for the groom's ring, although both rings may be selected at the same time.)

The bride comes down the aisle last, on her father's right arm. If her father cannot escort her down the aisle, a brother or other male relative may do so. The father should keep well to the left so there will be ample room for the bride's dress. (Some ministers prefer that the bride come down the aisle on the father's left arm so he can more easily put her hand into the hand of the groom.)

After all have reached the Communion rail, the arrangements will look like this:

Minister

☐	☐	☐	☐	☐	☐	☐	☐
Usher	Usher	Maid of Honor	Bride	Groom	Best Man	Usher	Usher

☐	☐	☐	☐	☐	☐	☐
Brides-maid	Brides-maid	Flower Girl	Bride's Father	Ring Bearer	Brides-maid	Brides-maid

When the bride and her father reach the foot of the chancel steps or the Communion rail, she releases his arm and steps forward, next to the groom. Some ministers request that the father place the bride's right hand in the hand of the minister, who then places her hand in the right hand of the groom. The entire bridal party now turns and faces the altar.

The father remains standing beside and one step to the rear of the bride until the minister says, "Who giveth this woman to be married to this man?" (The minister may use first names here.) The father answers, "I do." (Some fathers prefer to say, "Her mother and I do.") The bride then shifts her flowers to the left hand or gives them to the maid or matron of honor to hold so that her right hand will be free for the next part of the service. Her father sits down with her mother in the left front pew.

In churches with a divided chancel the minister may, at this point, lead the bride and groom and two attendants to the kneeling bench before the altar. Otherwise, the whole ceremony takes place before the Communion rail. The minister will tell the couple when to join hands and what to say, so they need not worry about this, even though they may have memorized the responses. The congregation does appreciate it if both bride and groom will respond audibly and distinctly. For that reason it is well to go over the responses both before and during the rehearsal.

If the bride is still holding her bouquet, she gives it to the bridesmaid so that her left hand will be free to receive the ring at the same time that the best man is giving the ring to the minister. The bridesmaid holds the flowers until the close of the ceremony.

After the Ceremony

With the last *Amen* following the benediction, the recessional march begins, and the bride takes her flowers from the bridesmaid, who raises the veil. If the bride wishes, the groom kisses her before she takes his right arm for the march up the aisle. They should walk, not run. People are eager to see how happy they look. The couple moves out the door to their car if they are leaving the church, or to the church parlors if a reception is to be held there.

The best man offers his right arm to the maid of honor and they follow. The ring bearer and flower girl come next, then the bridesmaids, walking with the ushers. Those on the left side as you face the altar will have to cross behind the bridesmaids so that each bridesmaid comes up the aisle on an usher's right arm.

Ushers should remember that as soon as they take the bridesmaids to the front door, they must return to usher out close relatives. The bride's mother leaves first, usually on an usher's arm, followed by the bride's father. Next the groom's mother is ushered out. The groom's father follows. Sometimes grandparents are also ushered out, but this is optional. Other guests leave without direction.

The ushers must now go to the reception. This procedure should be carefully planned so they will be sure to reappear when and where they are needed.

The Reception

After the wedding ceremony, if there is to be a reception, the bridal party goes immediately to the home of the bride or to the church parlor or other place arranged for it. In this day of small homes, the bride's family frequently arranges for the reception to be held at the church. Some church groups are accustomed to catering for receptions, but you may prefer to bring in an outside caterer or make other arrangements. The advantage of a church reception is that you can include everyone who attends the wedding ceremony.

Guests will be arriving soon after the bride and groom. Therefore it is important to organize the receiving line as quickly as possible. If photographs are to be made, the photographer should wait until after people have gone through the line rather than keep a large number of people waiting. Sometimes pictures are taken at the chancel following the ceremony while the reception is being prepared, but this takes the time of the guests. Clear all details with the photographer in advance. The purpose of a reception is to give people an opportunity to congratulate the bride and groom and to meet out-of-town members of the bridal party.

Again let us stress simplicity and sobriety. A few flowers for the tables and greens near the receiving line are all the decorations necessary. This is not a time to spend more than you can afford for elaborate decorations. Frequently the flowers are brought from the church and used for the reception.

Simple refreshments, such as punch and cake and possibly nuts, are all that are needed. People do not come to a reception to eat, but to meet the bride and groom. Alcoholic beverages should never be served at a reception in a United Methodist church.

The receiving line is generally arranged as follows: bride's mother, groom's father, groom's mother, bride's father, bride, groom, maid or matron of honor.

Bridesmaids may be included in the line, but they usually help serve refreshments. The bride's father may stand in the line, but some authorities on wedding etiquette feel he should be free to mingle with the guests. The groom's father should remain in line unless excused because of diffidence or illness. The best man and ushers do not usually participate in the receiving line. They mingle with guests, helping wherever they may be needed.

Special guests may be included in the receiving line, if desired. A grandmother or a visiting clergyman or distinguished guests whom the bride wishes to present to her friends may be included at her special invitation. This is her family's reception, and she can arrange it as she wishes.

People who come through the receiving line should be introduced. If the bride's mother does not know a person, she says, "I'm Mrs. ———," and the guest will usually respond by giving his name. She introduces him to the groom's father. Each person in the line then introduces the guest to the next in line. As guests leave the line, they are served refreshments.

After all the guests have been received, the bride and groom cut the cake, and refreshments are served to those in the receiving line. If the wedding cake is to be served to the guests, however, it should be cut earlier.

The bride and groom mingle with the guests for a few minutes before leaving to change clothes, but they should not delay too long because many of the guests are waiting to see them leave. The maid of honor goes with the bride to help her change. When the bride is ready, she sends for her parents and the parents of the groom so they can say good-bye to them before leaving on the honeymoon. It is not now considered good form for newlyweds to slip out the back way. The waiting guests want to see them leave and express good wishes for their happiness.

Summary

Whether you plan for a large wedding or a small one, you want it to be a reverent and memorable occasion. Careful planning takes time and work, but it is hoped that you will be married for a long time and careful attention to the details discussed in this chapter may help you avoid mistakes. Many traditions are associated with weddings. You need not observe all of them, but some of them will strengthen your marriage in the years ahead. They will be happy memories you can share together.

CHAPTER VII

Your Church Is Interested

This book has been prepared to help you get ready for one of the most important events in your life. Your church feels that adequate preparation for marriage is important, and your minister appreciates the opportunity to help you find answers to your questions.

Your friends in the church are hopeful that you will have the best possible marriage. They are ready to help you with your preparations, and they will be on call should you need help after your wedding.

Your minister will still be your friend and counselor too. Keep in touch with him. Share with him your joyous experiences as well as problems which may arise. Do not hesitate to turn to him for help at any time. If he cannot help you, he can probably refer you to someone who can. He is concerned that you remain happily married through the years. He may move to another community, and another minister may become the pastor of your church, but do not hesitate to ask for counsel at any time.

If you do have difficulty, most ministers would prefer to talk with both of you. If both are willing to come for counseling, this tells him that you are both concerned about your marriage. Nevertheless, it is better for one person to seek counseling than for neither to ask.

As you look ahead to years together, you may feel that you can meet any problem that may arise, but you will not be able to anticipate all of them. For example, some disagreements will center around the discipline of your children, which college they should attend, or how to pay for a college education.

Another group of problems will center around family relationships. It is not always possible to maintain a neutral relationship in treatment of your own parents. There may be times when one parent will need special attention or care, and the question of what to do about an aged or widowed parent may have to be faced. And just at the time when school expenses for your children are especially heavy, other members of the family may need help. There may be occasions, too, when there are unusually heavy financial pressures in the family, possibly when the breadwinner is out of work.

It is not possible or advisable to avoid all situations which you may find disturbing. Meet each problem as it comes, then try to find how best to deal with it. When illness or death comes, you cannot avoid these experiences. Accept them as a part of life. The acceptance of a grandparent into the home may be a disturbing influence in the family; on the other hand, it may prove a great blessing. One need not feel guilty, however, if he cannot accept this kind of a relationship and makes other provisions for his loved ones. Do not hesitate to

117

turn to your church for advice and counsel when any difficult circumstances arise.

Some couples may have bought homes that are too large and expensive for them to maintain. Drastic changes may be necessary at some time in the future if total living costs are to be met. Through your church you may be put in touch with a banker or financial advisor who will show you how to lighten your load.

In the adult groups of your church you will find opportunities to discuss religion, social action, family living, world outreach, and evangelism. Here you will be able to make new friendships with other couples. You will discover that they have similar difficulties and interests. You can find a depth of friendship in your church that will strengthen your life together and support you in meeting the challenge of everyday living.

Your church is more than an anchor in the storm. It offers opportunities for Christian growth. It will help you strengthen your family life; it will provide channels for service to your community and to the world. We hope you will accept and welcome the many opportunities which your church offers you.

May God's blessing be with you as you begin the adventure of marriage together.

OUR PRAYER

Our Father, in whom our life together has its roots, we give thee praise and thanksgiving for the holy union which you have given to us through the vows of marriage. Man and woman were created to fulfill and to complete the lives of each other, and we are awed and grateful that our paths have grown together so that we may have this new life.

Teach us the meaning of our marriage. May we continue to grow in love for each other and to deepen our understanding of each one's desires and needs. In our laughing together and in our crying together, and through faithfulness to each other, grant that we may learn what it means to love fully, to work diligently, to play wholeheartedly, to serve humbly, and to endure all things for the sake of each other.

But keep us from getting lost in ourselves, we pray. May the love we find together lead us to love others more completely. May our caring for each other and our children help us to care for others, so that the blessing of this union will make us servants of yours in the world.

We pray that the home we establish will be a fellowship filled with thy Spirit, for to thee be all the glory and praise. Amen.

—Margaret and Edward Geiger

119

The Order for the Service of Marriage

At the time appointed, the persons to be married, having been qualified according to the laws of the state and the standards of the Church, standing together facing the minister, the man at the minister's left hand and the woman at the right hand, the minister shall say,

Dearly beloved, we are gathered together here in the sight of God, and in the presence of these witnesses, to join together *this man and this woman* in holy matrimony; which is an honorable estate, instituted of God, and signifying unto us the mystical union which exists between Christ and his Church; which holy estate Christ adorned and beautified with his presence in Cana of Galilee. It is therefore not to be entered into unadvisedly, but reverently, discreetly, and in the fear of God. Into this holy estate these two persons come now to be joined. If any man can show just cause why they may not lawfully be joined together, let him now speak, or else hereafter forever hold his peace.

Addressing the persons to be married, the minister shall say,

I require and charge you both, as you stand in the presence of God, before whom the secrets of all hearts are disclosed, that, having duly considered the holy covenant you are about to make, you do now declare before this company your pledge of faith, each to the other. Be well assured that if these solemn vows are kept inviolate, as God's Word demands, and if steadfastly you endeavor to do the will of your heavenly Father, God will bless your marriage, will grant you fulfillment in it, and will establish your home in peace.

Then shall the minister say to the man, using his Christian name,

N., wilt thou have this woman to be thy wedded wife, to live together in the holy estate of matrimony? Wilt thou love her, comfort her, honor and keep her, in sickness and in health; and forsaking all other keep thee only unto her so long as ye both shall live?

The man shall answer,

I will.

Then shall the minister say to the woman, using her Christian name,

N., wilt thou have this man to be thy wedded husband, to live together in the holy estate of matrimony? Wilt thou love him, comfort him, honor and keep him, in sickness and in health; and forsaking all other keep thee only unto him so long as ye both shall live?

The woman shall answer,

I will.

Then shall the minister say,

Who giveth this woman to be married to this man?

The father of the woman, or whoever gives her in marriage, shall answer,

I do.

Then the minister, receiving the hand of the woman from her father or other sponsor, shall cause the man with his right hand to take the woman by her right hand, and say after him,

I, N., take thee, N., to be my wedded wife, to have and to hold, from this day forward, for better, for worse, for richer, for poorer, in sickness and in health, to love and to cherish, till death us do part, according to God's holy ordinance; and thereto I pledge thee my faith.

Then shall they loose their hands; and the woman, with her right hand taking the man by his right hand, shall say after the minister,

I, N., take thee, N., to be my wedded husband, to have and to hold, from this day forward, for better, for worse, for richer, for poorer, in sickness and in health, to love and to cherish, till death us do part, according to God's holy ordinance; and thereto I pledge thee my faith.

Then they may give to each other rings, or the man may give to the woman a ring, in this wise: the minister, taking the ring or rings, shall say,

The wedding ring is the outward and visible sign of an inward and spiritual grace, signifying to all the uniting of this man and this woman in holy matrimony, through the Church of Jesus Christ our Lord.

Then the minister may say,

Let us pray.

Bless, O Lord, the giving of these rings, that they who wear them may abide in thy peace, and continue in thy favor; through Jesus Christ our Lord. **Amen.**

Or, if there be but one ring, the minister may say,

Bless, O Lord, the giving of this ring, that he who gives it and she who wears it may abide forever in thy peace, and continue in thy favor; through Jesus Christ our Lord. **Amen.**

The minister shall then deliver the proper ring to the man to put upon the third finger of the woman's left hand. The man, holding the ring there, shall say after the minister,

In token and pledge of our constant faith and abiding love, with this ring I thee wed, in the name of the Father, and of the Son, and of the Holy Spirit. Amen.

Then, if there is a second ring, the minister shall deliver it to the woman to put upon the third finger of the man's left hand; and the woman, holding the ring there, shall say after the minister,

In token and pledge of our constant faith and abiding love, with this ring I thee wed, in the name of the Father, and of the Son, and of the Holy Spirit. Amen.

Then shall the minister join their right hands together and, with his hand on their united hands, shall say,

Forasmuch as N. and N. have consented together in

123

holy wedlock, and have witnessed the same before God and this company, and thereto have pledged their faith each to the other, and have declared the same by joining hands and by giving and receiving *rings*; I pronounce that they are husband and wife together, in the name of the Father, and of the Son, and of the Holy Spirit. Those whom God hath joined together, let not man put asunder. **Amen.**

Then shall the minister say,

Let us pray.

Then shall the husband and wife kneel; the minister shall say,

O eternal God, creator and preserver of all mankind, giver of all spiritual grace, the author of everlasting life: Send thy blessing upon this man and this woman, whom we bless in thy name; that they may surely perform and keep the vow and covenant between them made, and may ever remain in perfect love and peace together, and live according to thy laws.

Look graciously upon them, that they may love, honor, and cherish each other, and so live together in faithfulness and patience, in wisdom and true godliness, that their home may be a haven of blessing and a place of peace; through Jesus Christ our Lord. **Amen.**

Then the husband and wife, still kneeling, shall join with the minister and congregation in the Lord's Prayer, saying,

124

Our Father, who art in heaven, hallowed be thy name. Thy kingdom come, thy will be done on earth as it is in heaven. Give us this day our daily bread. And forgive us our trespasses, as we forgive those who trespass against us. And lead us not into temptation, but deliver us from evil. For thine is the kingdom, and the power, and the glory, forever. Amen.

Then the minister shall give this blessing:

God the Father, the Son, and the Holy Spirit bless, preserve, and keep you; the Lord graciously with his favor look upon you, and so fill you with all spiritual benediction and love that you may so live together in this life that in the world to come you may have life everlasting. Amen.

ADDITIONAL READING

For Engaged Couples

A Christian Interpretation of Marriage, by Henry A. Bowman. Philadelphia: Westminster Press, 1959.

Beginning Your Marriage, by Walter J. Imbiorski and John L. Thomas. Delaney Publications, 1966.

Being Married, by Evelyn M. Duvall and Reuben L. Hill. New York: Association Press, 1960.

Getting Ready for Marriage, by David R. Mace. Nashville: Abingdon Press, 1972.

Sex, Love and Marriage, Jules Saltman, Editor for Public Affairs Committee. New York: Grossett & Dunlap, 1968.

Sexual Harmony in Marriage, by Oliver M. Butterfield. New York: Emerson Books, Rev., 1967.

The Complete Book of Birth Control, by Alan F. Guttmacher. New York: Ballantine Books, 1961.

For Married Couples

After You've Said I Do, by Dwight Harvey Small. Old Tappan, N. J.: Fleming H. Revell, 1968.

Guideposts to Creative Family Worship, by Anna Laura and Edward W. Gebhard. Nashville: Abingdon Press, 1953.

How to Keep Romance in Your Marriage, by W. Clark Ellzey. New York: Association Press, 1965.

Inscape, by Ross Snyder. Nashville: Abingdon Press, 1968.

Sex in Marriage, New Understandings, by D. W. Baruch and Hyman Miller. New York: Harper & Row, 1962.

The Christian Family and Its Money, by David M. Graybeal. Board of Missions, The United Methodist Church.

Your First Year of Marriage, by Tom McGinnis. Garden City, N.Y.: Doubleday & Co., 1967.

Whom God Hath Joined, by David R. Mace. Philadelphia: Westminster Press, 1953.

College Texts

Building a Successful Marriage, by Judson T. and Mary G. Landis. Englewood Cliffs, N.J.: Prentice-Hall, 5th Ed., 1968.

Education for Marriage, by James A. Peterson. New York: Charles Scribner's Sons, 2nd Ed., 1964.

Making the Most of Marriage, by Paul H. Landis. New York: Appleton-Century-Crofts, 1970.

Marriage, by Robert O. Blood. New York: The Free Press, 2nd Ed., 1969.

Marriage for Moderns, by Henry A. Bowman. New York: McGraw-Hill. 6th Ed., 1970.

Books on Wedding Etiquette

Amy Vanderbilt's New Complete Book of Etiquette, by Amy Vanderbilt. Rev. Ed., Garden City, N.Y.: Doubleday & Co., 1963.

The Wedding Book, by Frances and Frederic A. Birmingham. New York: Harper & Row, 1964.

Wedding Information

(To be filled out by the couple together. Dates should be set in consultation with the minister.)

Woman's full name _____

Address _____

Telephone at work _____ Home _____

    Parents' Name _____

    Address _____

Man's full name _____

Address _____

Telephone at work _____ Home _____

    Parents' Name _____

    Address _____

Your address after wedding _____

_____

Dates for premarital conferences with minister: Couple ___

    Man _____ Woman _____ Couple _____

Dates for premarital conferences with physician:

    Man _____ Woman _____

    Physician's name _____

Have you secured the marriage license? _____

If not, when? _____

Rehearsal Date _____ Hour _____ Place _____

Rehearsal Dinner _____ Hour _____ Place _____

Wedding Date _____ Hour _____

Place _____

Maid of Honor _____

Best Man _____

Bridesmaids _____

_____

_____

_____

Ushers _____

_____

_____

_____

Other attendants: _____

_____

Who will give the bride in marriage? _____

Will you use one ring? _____ or two rings? _____

Where will the reception be held? _____

Organist _____

Soloist _____

Florist _____

Photographer _____